DATA ANALYSIS

- an applied guide for managers

Philippe Versijp

TO MY PARENTS

WITHOUT YOU, NONE OF IT WOULD HAVE BEEN POSSIBLE

ACKNOWLEDGEMENTS

I'd like to thank those who made this book possible, first and foremost my students in the MFM and XFM (now GEMFM) programs who gave valuable feedback on earlier drafts. Some advice I took, some I didn't, and I hope none of your many remarks slipped under the radar, but I'm grateful for all of it.

Likewise, I'd like to thank Jaap Spronk, Renny Maduro, Willem Verschoor, Jeroen Ligterink and Marc Roels for support or assistance in various ways - not in the least by creating possibilities.

Also, I'd like to thank Roger Lee at IHS for his contribution to obtaining the necessary permissions. All copyrights of the EVIEWS software and related trademarks belong to IHS. Screenshots used with permission.

Of course, any remaining errors are my own.

Contents:

Part I : Introduction

Intuitively, everyone in business knows that some things are related – such as your advertisement efforts and sales. Or one would hope they are related... While experience can often go a long way in establishing these kinds of relationships, it is desirable to have *evidence* for their existence. That involves analyzing data, and finding relationships among this data. Academic literature has developed many tools that can help with this job; this book contains a selection of them, tailored and explained in a way that is accessible for a broad professional audience. You, as reader, are given the tools to extract the information you need from the data.

However, crunching the numbers in a statistically sound way can be cumbersome and one is easily distracted by details. *In order to focus on the important aspects for as wide an audience as possible, I dispense with any unnecessary frills.* 'Data analysis' will therefore do nicely as the title for this book, as that's exactly what the topic is: how to get from real-life data to a relationship that contains useful information, on which you can act (does something, for example a new method to process orders, influence something else, such as cost). No urns with six white and three black balls or advanced econometrics, but simply estimating how a change in interest rates or advertising will affect your bottom line.

Of course, what is useful information depends on the audience. This book is written with a professional business audience in mind. However, it can be fruitful beyond the realm of managers, consultants and MBA students; anyone who regularly encounters problems on which numerical data is available should benefit from its contents. This book may also serve as additional literature for university and college students.

The 'no frills' approach also extends to the prerequisite knowledge. The material is presented at university level, yet to follow it you need no more math skills that addition, subtraction, division, multiplication, squares and square roots, and rearranging terms. I use calculus just once, and there's no need to study/refresh that topic for it.

In terms of its contents, the philosophy behind this book is that we're looking for *quantifiable* relationships: not just the presence of a relationship matters, but also how strong and how reliable it is. This assumption leads to a clear emphasis on *regression analysis* as our method of choice. While there are other methods to analyze data, those will not give the same possibilities of quantifying your results, or are in fact further developments of regression analysis. To explore those, the material in this book is indispensible for your preparation. Again, the focus is on the essentials.

You'll also notice that much of this book revolves around solving the *problems* encountered in data analysis. As a method, regression analysis is fairly simple, and sufficient for the vast majority of real-life problems. Yet, as Disraeli supposedly once said, there are "lies, damned lies and statistics". Due to the fact that no analysis of real world problems can ever be perfect, there is always some remaining uncertainty, and plenty of room for error. This uncertainty needs to be judged; maybe it casts doubt on your results, maybe not. Uncorrected, methodological errors can – and often do! – alter your conclusions completely. So a book on data analysis would not be worthwhile if it didn't include substantial sections on which problems you can expect, how to detect them, and above all, how to fix them. Only someone who mastered those aspects will be able to conduct meaningful analysis.

1. The important questions

Data analysis should serve a purpose, so the natural starting point is asking ourselves what we want to get out of it. The general problem is usually that we suspect there is some sort of relation between two phenomena / *variables*, and that we want to have a solid understanding of this relation, backed up by numbers. Does the relation exist, if so, how strong is it, and how reliable? For example, a manager would like to know the relation between profit and the cost of resources needed to make his or her product. Or the factors that drive the value of the company (did that new venture increase value?). Or the extent to which an investment portfolio is at risk due to changing exchange rates. The list is endless, but all of these problems share three important questions, which summarize the information we need from the data:

1. ## How strong is the relation?

    This also captures the existence of the relationship, moving from a strong relation to a weak one to none at all is simply a gradual change that can be summarized in changing a single number – and if the number is zero, no relation exists. For example, if we have data on advertisement expenditure and sales, we can formulate the relationship as follows (leaving out several parts for now):

    Sales (in Dollars or Euros) = b * Advertisement (in Dollars or Euros)

    The question is: what is this 'b'? Is it zero, and is there no relation? Is it 0.5, meaning that each dollar spent on advertisement only brings in 50 cents of additional sales (hardly good for your bottom line, in most cases), or is it 5 or even 20?

    Finding the strength of a relation lies at the core of each analysis.

2. How reliable are these numbers?

We may estimate that each dollar of advertisement brings in 12 dollars of sales, or that each unit of our new product will contribute a nice $1000,- tot our profits, but the person who later has to admit the real number is in fact zero, is unlikely to earn much favor in the boardroom. Even an error in the other direction does not reflect well on one`s skills. The conclusion is that we also want to know how *reliable* the numbers are: obviously, no estimate can be perfectly precise, but a margin from 0 to 2000 is a completely different story than a margin of 990 to 1010. We'll have to establish a measure of reliability to go along with the coefficient that captures the relation.

The customary way to do is, is by looking at the *standard error*, which will be explained in chapter 4.

3. Do we understand the whole mechanism?

There is no easier way to draw wrong conclusions than by looking at only a part of the picture. In the example above we didn't allow for sales independent of our advertising – both other factors leading to sales, or sales independent of any variable we have data on were ignored. This almost certainly causes distortions of our results – and biased numbers rarely lead to good decisions.

In order to be able to use our analysis, we need to understand the entire mechanism at work. Chapter 4 will discuss some indicators of how well our analysis explains reality.

And beyond

While the structure used to analyze data is fairly straightforward, there are lots of issues that can pose a problem when implementing these methods using real-life data. These issues - and their solutions - will be discussed from chapter 5 onwards. Each chapter will also be accompanied by references to webcasts that demonstrate and explain how to implement this material. At the end of the book, you'll find a glossary explaining the important terms, and an overview of diagnostic tests and when to use them.

2. The framework that will provide the answers

Saying that there is a relation between two variables (say, profit and value of a company) is not very precise; it leaves open too many possibilities such as the shape of the relation – a straight line, a curve... there are lots of possibilities. Figure 2.1 gives some examples; in all these cases we took data representing the change in value of a company and its profit (in millions), and tried to make sense of this data by drawing a line or curve to symbolize the relationship).

Figure 2.1
In each case profit (loss if negative) is plotted on the horizontal axis, and change in company value on the vertical axis. Each dot represents the realized values for one quarter. The solid lines are examples of possible relations between changes in company value and profit, each with a different shape.

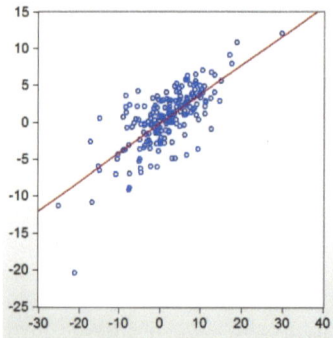

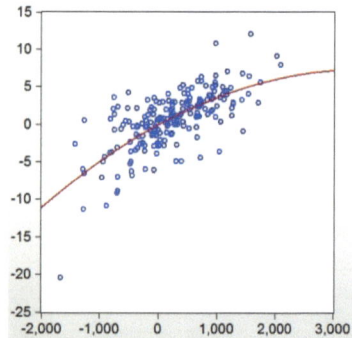

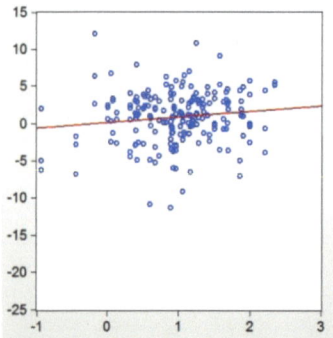

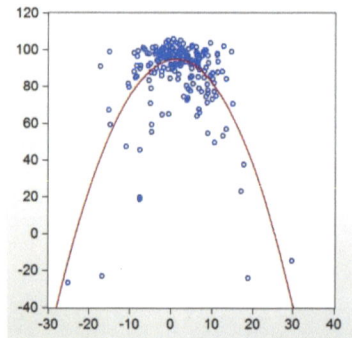

Also, graphical depictions don't say anything about cause and effect. And both verbal and graphical explanations become even more involved if we need to analyze how three or more variables interact.

A *formula* will however give a clear model of the relation between the *dependent variable* (the data we want to explain), commonly denoted with a Y, and one or more *independent variables* (the data which is assumed to represent the causes of changes in Y). The term independent signifies these variables are the ones that move others, rather than being influenced themselves (by any variable under investigation).

Independent variables are normally given the letter X, and if we have several, subscripts are used, such as X_1, X_2, X_3, to distinguish between the different variables. X_1 and X_2 are a whole lot shorter than 'sales in the north-western division' and 'euro-dollar exchange rate'. Additionally, we want to identify the individual observations that make up a variable (such as the euro-dollar exchange rate on January 2nd, 2015), for which we will employ the subscript t. (starting at 1, the beginning of the dataset, ending at T, representing the end date). For example, $X_{2,3}$ in the table below is -1.278:

Date	Subscript (t)	Value for Y	Value for X_1	Value for X_2
Jan 2nd	t=1	1.346	0.998	2.451
Jan 3rd	t=2	1.342	1.001	3.221
Jan 4th	t=3	1.353	0.976	-1.278
...	...	...	...	...
Jan 31st	t=T=30	1.221	0.567	4.060

We now need to combine these data in a formula – stipulating how these variables are related. The easiest choice is a linear relation: a straight line. (If that seems overly restrictive, see chapter 6 on how many alternatives can still be seen as a linear function). Examples are found in on the left hand side of Figure 2.1.

A typical formula for a linear relation is as follows:

$$y_t = a + b_1 X_{1,t} + b_2 X_{2,t} + e_t \tag{1}$$

You'll notice that besides the X and Y variables, you'll find an 'a', 2 b's and an e_t – this which makes equation 1 a more elaborate and vastly superior – model than the rudimentary one we saw in chapter 1.

The 'a' is called the *intercept* – it's a constant. Its role is to provide flexibility; if we remove the constant (or in fact set it equal to zero) that would mean that if both $X_{1,t}$ and $X_{2,t}$ are zero, Y_t must be zero too. That may be a poor description of reality, for example X_1 and X_2 could be units sold of two different types, and Y would be cost. As a company always has certain costs, even if production is zero, we need this constant to reflect this fact. The intercept causes the line to shift up and down depending on its value, providing flexibility in a vertical direction.

b_1 and b_2 are called *slope coefficients*, and they in fact answer the first major question: how strong is the relation? Does an additional unit increase costs by 5 or by 50? Or, as another example, is the influence of an exchange rate -5, 0 or +10? As the slope coefficients give the influence of the x-variables on y, these are the numbers we'll need to find. We'll have one for each variable.

Lastly, the e_t - the *residuals* - reflect the fact that no set of real-world data will perfectly fit a mathematical model like this. There will always be errors in your data, people or phenomena not behaving according to the model you stipulate, as well as random fluctuations. As each observation may have a different error due to these effects, we allow different values for e for each period, hence the use of e_t.

To sum it up, have a look at Figure 2.2. It contains X, Y, a and b. e would be the distance between the individual dots (observations) and the straight line, but for the sake of clarity the individual observations and the residuals have been omitted from this figure.

Figure 2.2

A stylized figure depicting x (the independent variable), y (the dependent variable, the one we seek to explain), the intercept a and the slope b.

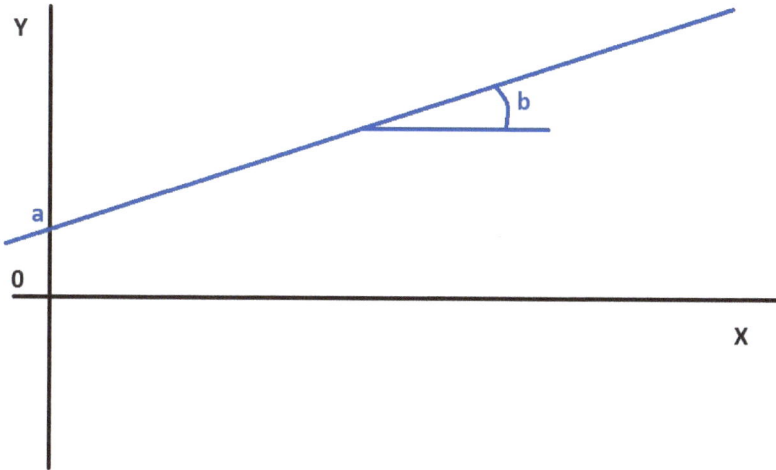

2.1. How do we find those numbers?

When we start our analysis, we only have our data, and no clue what the values of a and b (intercept and slope coefficients) are. We need to calculate those for the data we do have. Suppose for now that there is just one variable that we'll use to explain the other, so we have nothing more than two series of numbers, Y and X_1.

How the job at hand is how we're going to transform those numbers into the ones we really want to know, namely a and b_1?

The easiest strategy is to use what's called *Ordinary Least Squares* (OLS) regression. We'll leave the actual number-crunching to a computer, but it is very useful to see what happens inside this black box – it will help our understanding of problems down the road.

In a nutshell, we find the coefficients a and b_1 that produce the lowest (modified) errors, and, since the lowest possible errors are assumed to come from the best possible description of the data, those coefficients will be used as our estimates. *Now that sounds probably pretty vague still, so let's work through a step-by-step explanation.*

Step one starts with a formula, where we identify what we need to know (a and b_1 – the same applies to models with more independent variables and therefore slope-coefficients b_2, b_3 etcetera, but that's just excess notation for now), and allow for the possibilities of errors. So we have eq. 1 again.

$$y_t = a + b_1 X_{1,t} + e_t$$

Step two is to isolate the errors. We want a model that has the *lowest* possible errors, after all; lower errors are indicating a better explanation of the data. This is just rearranging terms.

$$e_t = y_t - a - b_1 X_{1,t}$$

Step three is to decide how to balance all those errors. Remember, it's e_t – we have an error for each observation, and we need to balance them, so we can compare different models (that is, different values for a and b_1) and decide which one is best.

This means, among other things, we have to decide if twenty errors which have all values around 2 are as bad as a single observation with value 40. Generally, the latter is seen as worse; bigger errors are much less likely to be the result of some random disturbances that are ultimately irrelevant, and more likely to indicate there's something seriously wrong with our model. This is why big errors should have a higher weight in translating that series of errors to one number that indicates the quality of the model.

Another issue is that errors can be both positive and negative, and that we don't want them to cancel out. A model with errors of zero is much better than a model with half the errors at -10 and the other half at +10. A solution to both these issues is to take the square of the errors (multiply each individual error by itself), and then add all these squared values. It's not the only possible solution, but it is by far the most convenient one. So we'll multiply each error with itself (this means negative numbers become positive), and add the result for each observation t. We then get the *sum of squared errors*. In mathematical notation:

$$Sum\ of\ squared\ errors = SSE = e_1^2 + e_2^2 + \cdots + e_T^2 = \sum_{t=1}^{t=T} e_t^2$$

Step four is then finding the numbers for a and b_1 that minimize this sum of squared errors. To do this, we use a result from calculus called the first order condition. If one takes the first derivative of an equation and sets it equal to zero, you find a maximum or a minimum of that function. Basic calculus allows us to prove that in this case we find a minimum, so we have the lowest possible sum of squared errors that can be obtained by varying the values of a and b_1 (our parameters). This minimum gives us two equations in two unknowns that can be rearranged to provide expressions for our intercept-coefficient a and slope coefficient b_1.

$$SSE = \sum_{t=1}^{t=T} e_t^2 = \sum_{t=1}^{t=T} (y_t - a - b_1 x_{1t})^2$$

$$= \sum_{t=1}^{t=T} (y_t^2 - 2ay_t - 2b_1 x_{1t} y_t + a^2 - 2ab_1 x_{1t} + b^2 x_{1t}^2)^2$$

So now we know what to minimize. The solution (the minimum) can be derived from teh first order conditions, which are as follows:

$$\frac{\partial SSE}{\partial a} = -2 \sum_{t=1}^{t=T} y_t + 2na - 2b_1 \sum_{t=1}^{t=T} x_{1,t} = 0$$

$$\frac{\partial SSE}{\partial b_1} = -2\sum_{t=1}^{t=T} x_{1,t} y_t + 2b_1 \sum_{t=1}^{t=T} x_{1,t}^2 - 2a \sum_{t=1}^{t=T} x_{1,t} = 0$$

That doesn't look too good, but let's combine and rearrange the terms in these equations, and drop the t's for so we get a less cumbersome notation. Then we get expressions for a and b_1.

$$b = \frac{\sum x_1 y + \sum x_1 \sum y}{\sum x_1^2 \, (\sum x_1)^2}$$

$$a = \frac{1}{n}\sum y + \frac{b}{n}\sum x_1 = \frac{1}{n}\sum y + \frac{1}{n}\frac{\sum x_1 y + \sum x_1 \sum y}{\sum x_1^2 \, (\sum x_1)^2}\sum x_1$$

Now these expressions still look somewhat horrible, but on the upside we should realize two things: firstly, all of these numbers can be expressed in sums, squares and averages and will at any rate be calculated by a PC, and secondly, the hard work is done - also in terms of algebraic formulas.

We have found a way to produce the numbers we're looking for; we now can find out how much our advertisement contributes to our sales or how profitable a new product is (to continue the earlier examples). Again, this gives us the first important piece of information, namely how strong the relationship is. However, we still have to figure out how reliable it is, and if we're missing important parts.

Before we go on with that, we'll first deal with how to produce these numbers from actual data; these calculations are best done on a PC, and since we later on will benefit enormously from specialized software, it's best to familiarize yourself with a tailor-made program.

Part II : Understanding the model

Thus far, we've got an outline of what we want to know, and the basics of how we're going to get that information from a dataset. But the formulas of chapter two involve tedious calculations, so the first step is to get acquainted with software that will help us implement the model. Once we have an understanding of how we perform this analysis, it is time to interpret the output. What are the answers to the important questions?

in reality, getting the right answers is something that will take several attempts, as not all data is easily captured in a regression model. Sometimes we need to employ additional 'tricks' to make sure the data can be properly analyzed in the first place. understanding the model means not just getting a computer to crunch the numbers, but also understanding what constitutes quality inputs.

3. Getting the numbers: EVIEWS

To get actual numbers for your slope and intercept coefficients – as well as loads of other info, much of which we'll also need later on – we need a computer and some software. In principle, a spreadsheet like Excel can do the job of finding the coefficients. However, many of the problems and solutions to those problems we'll encounter are very hard to implement in a spreadsheet. It is therefore strongly recommended you use specialized software. The *EVIEWS* program in particular is very well suited to regression analysis and the tasks at hand. It takes an initial investment to familiarize yourself with it, yet this investment will repay itself handsomely: many remedies will require just two clicks of the mouse.

Importing your data.

First of all, we need to get your data imported into EVIEWS. This is quite easy, if some simple preparation is done in a spreadsheet. Ideally, you lay out your data as follows: the first row contains short, descriptive names of all your variables (such as 'sales'), the first column the observations (for example sorted by period). See Figure 3.1.

Figure 3.1

	A	B	C	D	E
1		WTI	VIX	Market	Size_portfolio
2	1986-01-01	22,945	18,07	0,43	-0,76
3	1986-02-01	15,442	19,58	6,75	6,94
4	1986-03-01	12,618	21,59	4,79	5,33
5	1986-04-01	12,847	24,7	-1,32	-1,55
6	1986-05-01	15,444	21,92	4,60	4,83
7	1986-06-01	13,469	18,28	0,91	1,34
8	1986-07-01	11,575	17,85	-6,49	-5,43
9	1986-08-01	15,092	19,38	6,18	6,77
10	1986-09-01	14,913	18,61	-8,37	-9,53
11	1986-10-01	14,852	24,88	4,48	4,88
12	1986-11-01	15,207	19,23	1,13	2,23
13	1986-12-01	16,076	19,24	-3,14	-2,78
14	1987-01-01	18,656	18,79	12,42	12,98
15	1987-02-01	17,726	23,44	4,33	3,04
16	1987-03-01	18,305	22,86	1,86	2,24
17	1987-04-01	18,643	22,88	-2,15	-1,28
18	1987-05-01	19,415	28,22	0,14	0,53
19	1987-06-01	20,034	22,4	3,90	4,63
20	1987-07-01	21,355	20,99	3,95	3,82

I'll use this example throughout this chapter. The aim is to explain the returns on the 'size portfolio' (an investment portfolio based on a certain strategy) using a broad index of stocks (market), an index for the level of 'unrest' in the markets (VIX) and oilprices (WTI).

14

Now EVIEWS can import such a file from any spreadsheet application, or a .txt file. Choose the option 'Open Foreign data as Workfile'.

Figure 3.2

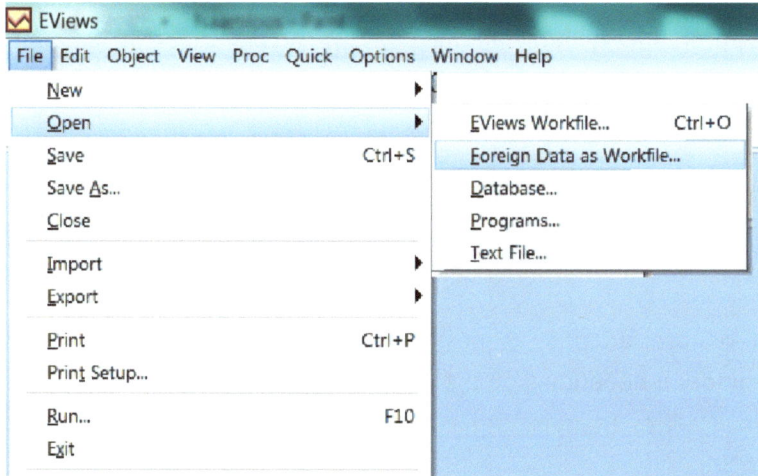

With a layout as described, one can click on 'finish' immediately; otherwise adjustments (for example in the number of rows used for headers) are possible. The result is a *workfile* in EVIEWS:

Figure 3.3

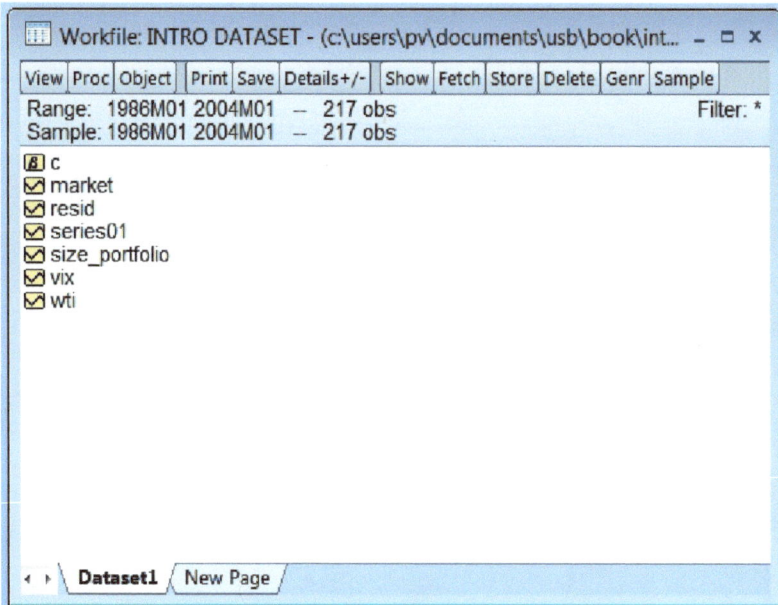

This workfile lists each variable (each column of the imported file) separately. Columns without a header are given names starting with 'series01'; in this case this refers to column A in Figure 3.1, which contained the date for each observation. It can be safely removed, as EVIEWS automatically detected the dates, as can been seen in Figure 3.3 after 'range' (all data available; 1986M01 denotes January 1986) and Sample (the data currently analysed).

Double-clicking on any series will open it in a spread-sheet view, with options to study the data: under 'view' you find options that produces descriptive statistics or graphs. See Figure 3.4.

NB: EVIEWS uses adaptive menus; the same button may have different options under it depending on the type of element we opened; the view menu in a series (marked 'A') is different from that in the workfile (marked 'B').

Figure 3.4

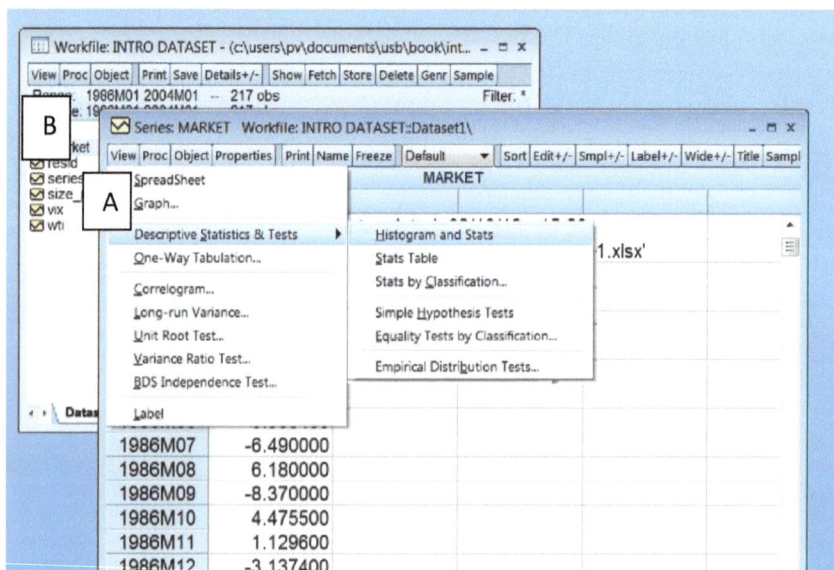

16

Run a regression

In order to run a regression, we go to the main menu, and under 'quick' choose 'estimate equation'.

Figure 3.5

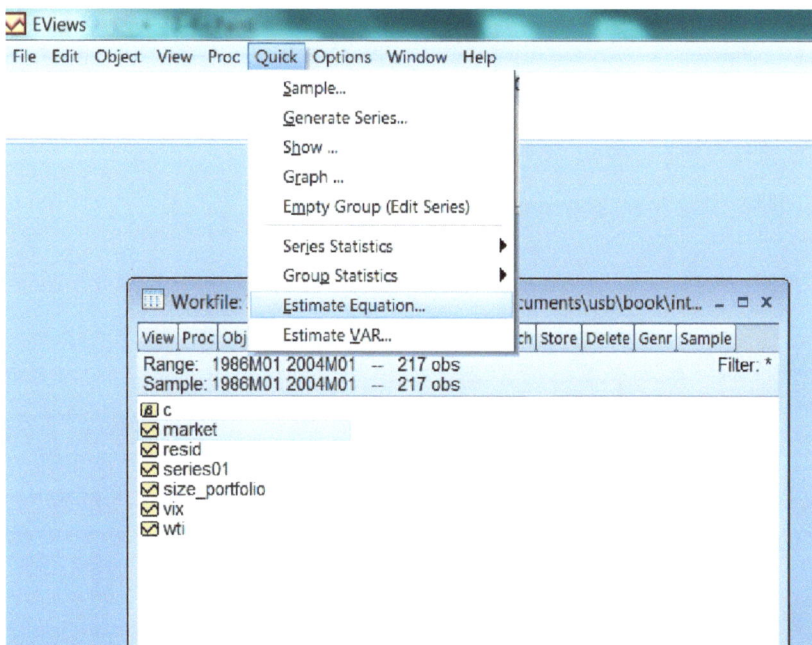

In this window we can enter our model, that is, we have to enter the equation we want to estimate. This can be done in two ways: the easiest is just a list of the variables, separated by spaces and with the dependent variable first, followed by a c to indicate the intercept, and then the names of the independent variables as they appear in your workfile. For example:

size_portfolio c market vix wti

This would give us the equation:

$$Size\_portfolio_t = a + b_1 market_t + b_2 VIX_t + b_3 WTI_t + e_t$$

In this dataset, t starts in January 1986, and ends with January 2004. Note that the residuals never have to be added to the equation in EVIEWS, the program always assumes there are residuals and adds them automatically.

While this method generally works well, typing out the equation in more detail is advisable: it allows you more control and will give you more insight into what is happening. In that case, the order remains the same, but each coefficient has to be mentioned explicitly. EVIEWS always uses the notation C(1), C(2), etc. for the coefficients, so the equation becomes:

Size_portfolio=c(1)+c(2)*market+c(3)*VIX+x(4)*WTI.

Figure 3.6

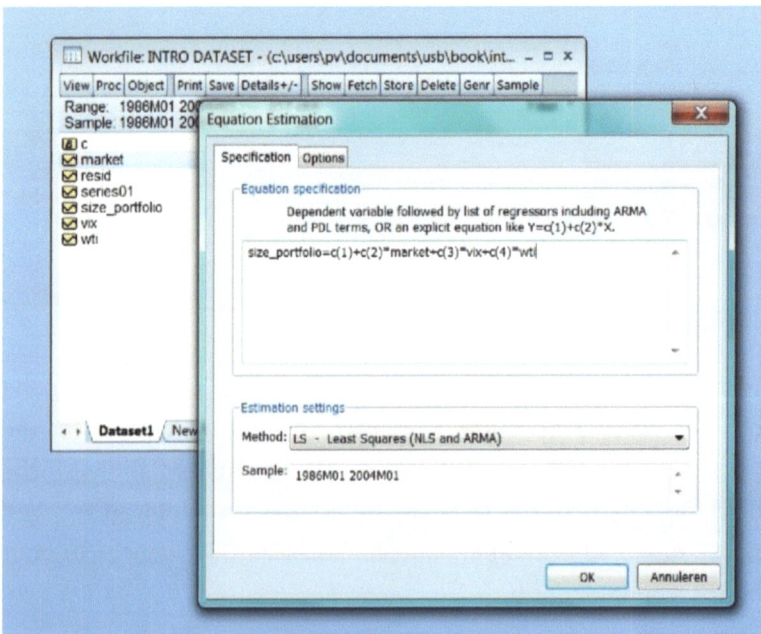

The equation will be estimated the moment one presses 'OK', for a standard OLS no additional options are needed, it's the default setting. The result will then look as follows:

Figure 3.7

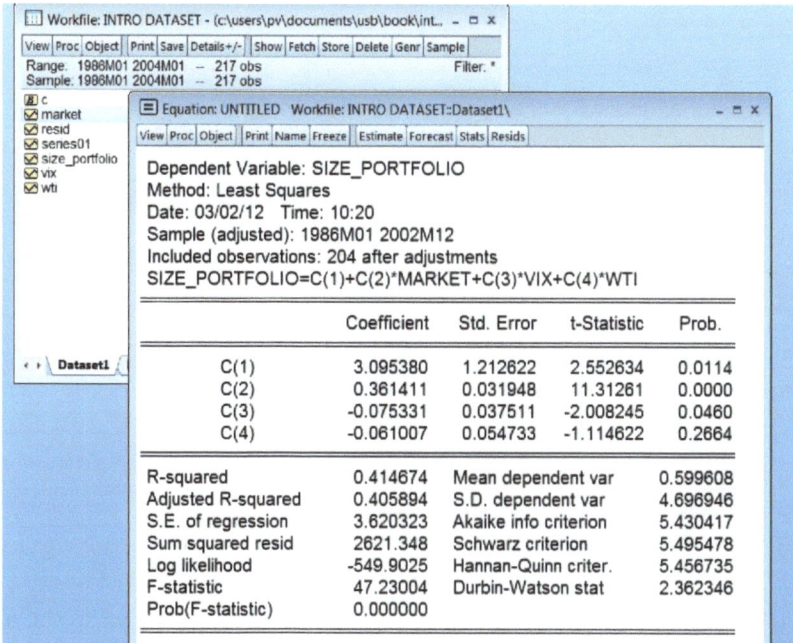

This equation can be saved by clicking the 'name' button. It's strongly advised to do this, otherwise a new estimation will overwrite the old one. You'll be prompted to provide a name for the equation, which will appear in your workfile. Spaces are not allowed in equation names.

The resulting output, an example of which you can find in Figure 3.8, merits closer analysis, which will be the topic of the next chapter.

Figure 3.8

```
Dependent Variable: SIZE_PORTFOLIO
Method: Least Squares
Date: 02/29/12   Time: 23:40
Sample (adjusted): 1986M01 2002M12
Included observations: 204 after adjustments
SIZE_PORTFOLIO=C(1)+C(2)*MARKET+C(3)*VIX+C(4)*WTI
```

	Coefficient	Std. Error	t-Statistic	Prob.
C(1)	3.095380	1.212622	2.552634	0.0114
C(2)	0.361411	0.031948	11.31261	0.0000
C(3)	-0.075331	0.037511	-2.008245	0.0460
C(4)	-0.061007	0.054733	-1.114622	0.2664

R-squared	0.414674	Mean dependent var	0.599608
Adjusted R-squared	0.405894	S.D. dependent var	4.696946
S.E. of regression	3.620323	Akaike info criterion	5.430417
Sum squared resid	2621.348	Schwarz criterion	5.495478
Log likelihood	-549.9025	Hannan-Quinn criter.	5.456735
F-statistic	47.23004	Durbin-Watson stat	2.362346
Prob(F-statistic)	0.000000		

NB: while in written formulas, we always tend to use X_1, X_2 and so on, in EVIEWS it is highly recommended to use a short abbreviation, such as 'market', 'VIX' or 'WTI'. The names are not case-sensitive.

Webcasts

Through www.covariance.nl you can find a series of webcasts that will help you with EVIEWS. Relevant webcasts for this chapter are:

1. Importing data

2. Restructuring a workfile

3. Estimating an equation

4. Interpreting your answers

Now we've got the standard regression output, the next step is to interpret these results. We'll start with the top half of Figure 3.8, namely the coefficients, standard errors, t-score and p-values. This will already allow us to answer the question if we have a relationship that can be relied upon – i.e., one that will survive the test of 'reasonable doubt'.

Coefficients and standard errors

In EVIEWS notation, a regression has the form Y=c(1)+c(2)*X; remember that the error term is assumed to be there automatically. The coefficients indicate the strength of the effects caused by X (of which there might be one, in which case we look at c(2), or several, in which case the slope coefficients are c(2), c(3) and c(4), such as in Figure 3.8) and those not caused by X (the intercept, c(1) in Figure 3.8).

These are the numerical answers that we're looking for.

We can also put these in a graph, after all, a linear equation is just the mathematical representation of a straight line! The intercept is the distance between the origin (coordinates 0,0) and the place where the line crosses the vertical axis; it gives us the estimated value of y if all independent variables would be zero. The slope-coefficient determines the gradient; a higher coefficient means a steeper line.

Figure 4.1 graphs the effects of the return on the market-index on the returns of the size-portfolio, based on the results in Figure 3.8. However, since there are three independent variables in that equation, we'd need a 4-dimensional graph! Since that's impossible, we ignore the effects of the VIX and WTI variables in this graph.

Figure 4.1

Size_portfolio (dependent variable)

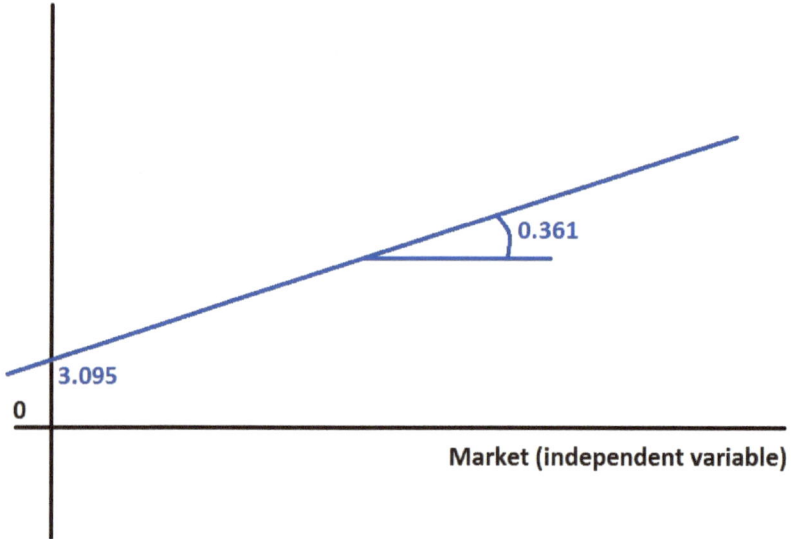

So while we have mapped the relationship between the size and market variables and obtained the numbers we set out to find, we're not done yet – the coefficients say very little by themselves, as OLS only guarantees it's the best estimate it can find, which is *not* the same as a *good* estimate *for our purposes*. Since no real life dataset will match a model perfectly, we need to keep in mind the possibility that the true numbers are not the ones we found. There's a level of uncertainty associated with our coefficients; due to chance, poor data or errors we may have found a stronger or weaker relation than really exists.

Luckily we have a way to judge and quantify this level of uncertainty. (Like OLS itself, this depends on a number of assumptions, to be discussed in Part III. If those assumptions are not met, the remedies of chapters 8-12 will be required). The number that indicates how (un)reliable a coefficient is, is its *standard error*. A high standard error indicates an unreliable coefficient, a low standard error a reliable one. This is why EVIEWS reports the standard errors directly behind each coefficient. Now two questions emerge: when is a standard error low enough, and what determines it?

We'll start with the latter question.

What drives standard errors?

Standard errors are a measure of reliability; if we want to have reliable estimates, we need low standard errors, and there are four factors that influence them. Controlling for these four (three are discussed in this subsection, the fourth in chapter 5) will allow you to improve the quality of your analysis, simply by avoiding unreliable results as much as possible.

The standard error, in case we have a regression *with a single independent variable* (so y = a + b*x +e) is calculated as follows:

$$S.E.= \sigma = \sqrt{\frac{\sigma_\varepsilon^2}{n\sigma_x^2}}$$

What are these three elements, σ_ε^2 , n and σ_x^2?

The first is the variance – denoted with sigma square, or σ^2, of the residuals. Variance is a measure of spread around the mean, and the mean (average) of the residuals is zero – see chapter 6. So the larger this variance, the more your residuals deviate from (their ideal value of) zero, and the worse your model fits the data. So this aspect kicks in the open door that in order to get reliable results, you need a model that describes the data well. Most of the time you can improve your model by adding relevant variables. We'll discuss practical advice on this in chapter 8. Figure 4.2 shows two situations: one model with small residuals (and therefore low variance of the residuals), another with high residuals. In the first case we can be reasonable sure about the slope of our line, in the second many different slopes seem almost equally plausible – and the calculations confirm that the slope coefficient is much more uncertain, as shown by its higher standard error.

Figure 4.2

Left, a model with a good fit, it is clear that the slope-coefficient of 1.21 is quite reliable (the line could be a bit steeper or less steep, but not much), the standard error is 0.09. Right, a poor fit. The slope-coefficient is -0.33, but the high standard error (relative to the coefficient) of 0.32 suggests a lot of different values for the slope could also be plausible - and hence the coefficient is unreliable.

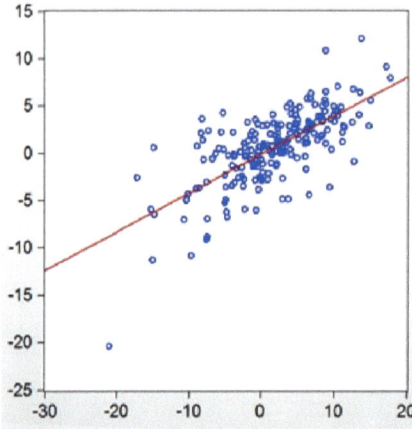

Good fit;
slope coefficient 1.21, st. err. 0.09

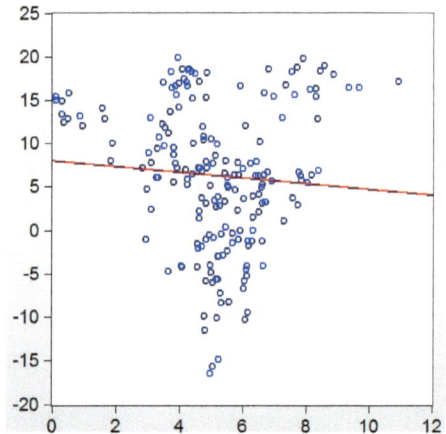

Poor fit;
slope coefficient -0.33, st. err. 0.32

The second element is n, which denotes the number of observations. It is easier to achieve reliable results if they are reached by incorporating lots of data, as the influence of a single random error or big deviation is smaller, and you simply have more information; see Figure 4.3.

Figure 4.3

A lower number of observations increases the standard error, in this we go from over 200 observations to less than 100, increasing the standard error from 0.026 to 0.035. Also visually, it is clear that the regression line in the right panel could more easily have a different slope than in the left panel.

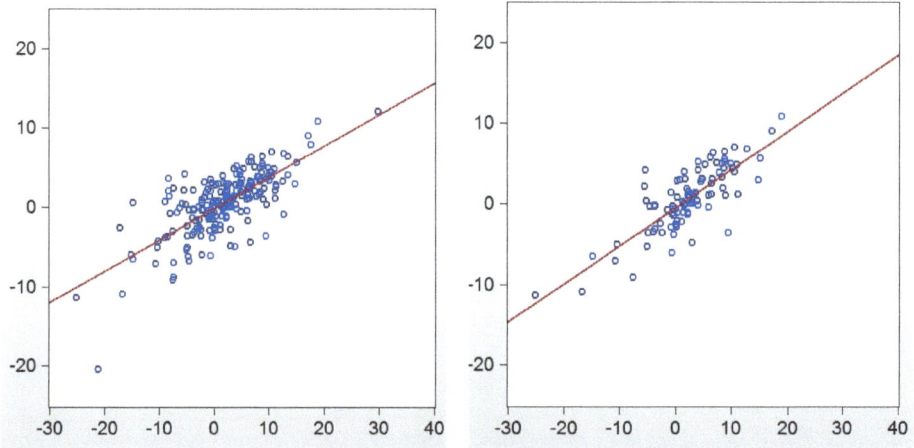

The third factor is the variance of your independent variable, σ_x^2. Again, variance is the spread of a variable around it's mean, but the value of the mean doesn't matter much here – what we want is that X assumes different values, and the variance measures this nicely. The reason you want x to assume different values is that we need to find a slope coefficient. The slope is nothing else than change in the vertical direction (Y) per unit of horizontal change (X) (see Figure 4.4); if X remains pretty much the same all the time, we have trouble finding out how Y moves in response, *as there's hardly any movement to respond to.*

Figure 4.4 illustrates that if all observations are clustered together, you could draw pretty much any line trough it without the fit noticeably worsening – in the panel on the right, a vertical line or a horizontal line seems to be equally well supported by the data, yet a vertical line implies a slope coefficient that approaches an infinitely large value, while a horizontal line represents a coefficient of zero – no relation at all! In panel the panel on the left the spread in the independent variable is much higher, and we now clearly have a moderately positive relation between X and Y.

Figure 4.4

If the range of the data is limited (the panel on the right depicts a subset of the data in the left part), it is very hard to obtain reliable values for a slope-coefficient, without calculations, it's hardly possible to tell if the slope should be positive or negative!

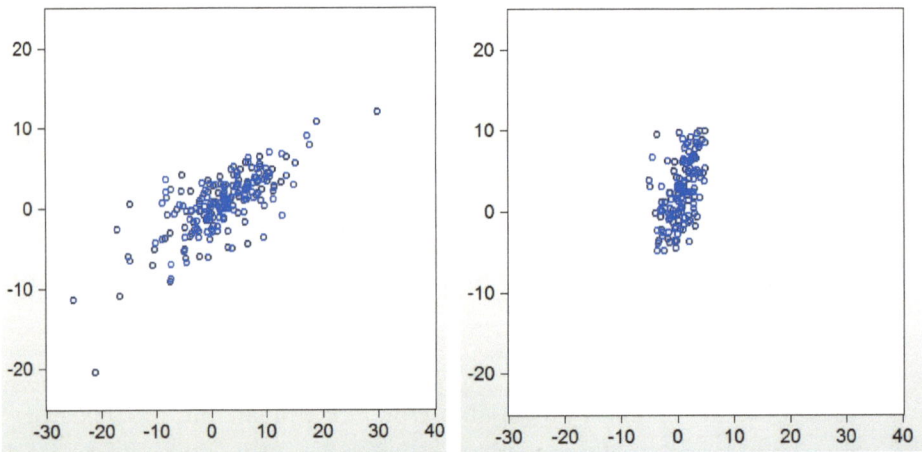

When is a standard error low enough? – the T-test and p-value

The other main question was how low a standard error actually has to be before we can call our results reliable. The answer depends on the value of the coefficient as the standard error can be seen as a margin of error of sorts: a large number – a strong relation - can survive a bigger margin of error before we question the validity of the relation. But we can be more precise, and attach a probability to the existence of a relation. This is done by means of a *hypothesis test*; the most basic form of these tests is the so-called t-test.

The idea behind a t-test is that we judge if the data provides enough evidence *against* a certain condition (for example our slope-coefficient being zero; this condition is called the *null-hypothesis*) so that we can – beyond any reasonable doubt – reject this condition.

At first, this negative formulation may be counter-intuitive; don't we want to prove that a relation exists, instead of ruling out there is none? The reason the second approach is chosen is almost philosophical: it is impossible to prove a coefficient has a certain value if we don't have a complete dataset (and we never have, not all possibilities materialize), but it is possible to state that some values are *highly unlikely* given the evidence we do have.

This is the 'beyond reasonable doubt' criterion referred to above; if we have a value for our slope- coefficient we know the strength of the relation, and we next want to make sure that this number isn't going to be zero (indicating the absence of a relation). So if we can reject this null-hypothesis, we can be reasonably sure that the relation exists as indicated by our model.

$$t - score = \frac{coefficient - value\ under\ null - hypothesis}{standard\ error\ of\ the\ coefficient}$$
$$= \frac{b - H_0}{\sigma_b}$$

The larger the t-score, the bigger the distance between the value of the null-hypothesis and the value we found; and therefore the likelihood of the null-hypothesis being true decreases.

Based on statistical theory we can attach a probability to these t-scores. For example, if we have a very large dataset (say, more than 200 observations), a t-score of 1.96 means there is just a 5% probability that we find a result like this if the true value would be zero. If the t-score is around 3, that probability drops to 1%. This probability is also called *a p-value* or *probability* and is reported under that name by EVIEWS.

Customarily we say we reject the null-hypothesis if the probabilities are so low. The chances of reaching an erroneous conclusion are so low we discount them. It should be noted that this 'beyond reasonable doubt' standard is customarily applied at probabilities below 10%, 5% or 1%. (Probably higher percentages than the legal profession would accept to go along with the same term). The choice of this threshold – or *significance level* – is up to the analyst. We'll use 5% in this book unless stated otherwise. Often, the p-value itself is reported as well so the reader can judge for himself; being able to report a p-value of 0.0000 is often seen as more convincing – and is so, if no mistakes have been made.

And the regression as a whole?

While it is good to have reliable coefficients, for certain purposes – such as forecasting – it is also necessary that the model as a whole performs well; in other words, that the combination of various independent variables explains the dependent variable with a high degree of accuracy.

An indicator of quality of the entire model is given by the R^2 *(R-squared) statistic*. It is based on the sum of squared residuals, the same measure that OLS minimizes. The formula is as follows:

$$R^2 = \frac{\Sigma e_t^2}{\Sigma (y_t - \bar{y})^2}$$

where $\bar{y}$ stands for the average of y. This means that a model with a perfect fit – all residuals are zero – will have an R^2 of one. If the model doesn't explain anything at all, the R^2 will be zero, since the fitted model will be a horizontal straight line with intercept equal to the average value of the y-variable. In that case the residuals are equal to the deviations in y from its average, so numerator and denominator are equal, so the R^2 just becomes 1-1 = 0. Because the R^2 should have a value between zero and one, it's often quoted as a percentage – the percentage of the movement in y that your model can explain.

Obviously, a higher R^2 indicates a better model, but there are no absolute thresholds. In explaining (volatile) high frequency financial markets data you expect a lower R^2 than when plotting factory output, as the former has a lot more influences we can never hope to incorporate in our model. Moreover, even a very low R^2 – even one below 1% - can still lead to coefficients that are significant. It therefore depends on the purpose of your model what your R^2 should be:

- If your conclusions can be drawn based on the coefficients only, the R^2 is of no importance, except relatively; if you have a competing model which produces a higher R^2, that is in general the better model.
- If your model is designed to forecast a variable, nothing beats experience in your particular branch or field. Thresholds will vary according to industry practice. Yet an R^2 below 50% means you understand less than half of the movements you seek to forecast, which would make such a model an extremely hard sale to a critical audience, unless the audience understands it's hardly possible to achieve such a number for that particular problem (for example, when forecasting financial markets).

Webcasts

Through www.covariance.nl you can find a series of webcasts that will help you with EVIEWS. Relevant webcasts for this chapter are:

4. Interpreting the output of a regression

Appendix: overview of the interpretation of EVIEWS output

When running a regression, your standard output will look like this:

Dependent Variable: SIZE_PORTFOLIO a.
Method: Least Squares
Date: 02/29/12   Time: 23:40
Sample (adjusted): 1986M01 2002M12 b.
Included observations: 204 after adjustments c.
SIZE_PORTFOLIO=C(1)+C(2)*MARKET+C(3)*VIX+C(4)*WTI d.

h.

	Coefficient	Std. Error	t-Statistic	Prob.
C(1) e.	3.095380	1.212622	2.552634	0.0114
C(2)	0.361411	0.031948	11.31261	0.0000
C(3)	-0.075331	0.037511	-2.008245	0.0460
C(4)	-0.061007	0.054733	-1.114622	0.2664

R-squared i.	0.414674	Mean dependent var	0.599608
Adjusted R-squared	0.405894	S.D. dependent var	4.696946
S.E. of regression	3.620323	Akaike info criterion	5.430417
Sum squared resid	2621.348	Schwarz criterion	5.495478
Log likelihood	-549.9025	Hannan-Quinn criter.	5.456735
F-statistic	47.23004	Durbin-Watson stat	2.362346
Prob(F-statistic)	0.000000		

j.   f.   g.

Important elements are:

a. Your dependent variable, the data you want to explain.

b. The sample: which data is used to calculate these results.

c. Number of observations (denoted n or t in most formulas) that are used; EVIEWS skips observations for which one of the variables involved has a missing value.

d. The formula, in a format EVIEWS understands. Market, VIX and WTI are independent variables here. NB: the residual is automatically added, and not displayed, except in the resid series.

e. Coefficients - the intercept [C(1)] and slope coefficients [C(2), C(3) and C(4)], which give you the best estimate of the relation between independent variables and the dependent variable. Note that a low absolute value may not say much: the coefficient for VIX is -0.006, but the average value for VIX is 40. -0.006*40 = -0.24, which may still contribute quite a bit. In this case, the estimated model is:

Size10 = 0.7865 + 0.9708*market - 0.006*VIX - 0.028*WTI

f. The standard errors of the coefficients. They indicate how reliable the coefficients are: a high standard error means there's much uncertainty about the true value of the coefficient.

g. t-statistic: element of a hypothesis test (t-test) with null-hypothesis that the corresponding coefficient is zero. The higher it is, the less likely the null-hypothesis. Calculated by taking the coefficient, substract zero (value null-hypothesis) and divide by the standard error.

h. Probability: the chance of finding these values if the null (coefficient is zero) is true.

If this is below 5%, we reject the null-hypothesis. If we reject the null, the corresponding coefficient is not zero, and this variable is significant (it has a significant influence on your dependent variable). It then should remain in the model. If the probability is above 5%, there is not enough evidence to reject the null, the coeficient may be zero and can be removed from the model if you so desire. For this output, that means the following:

- prob C(1) = 0.037; that's lower than 5%, so the null is rejected: our intercept is significant; it is not zero.
- prob C(2) = 0.000; again lower than 5%, null-hypothesis (i.e., ceoff = 0) is rejected, the coeff. [0.9708] is significant, which means that the market helps to explain the size10 returns, afterall, if the coefficient would be zero (it's not!) market would have no influence, it would drop out since you would

multiply all values by zero. Now we keep market in the model, its coefficient is 0.97.

- prob C(3) = 0.572, this is higher than 5%; we do not reject the null; the coefficient is so unreliabel its value could be zero, it's not significant, it can be removed from the model. VIX does not help us explain Size10.
- prob. C(4) = 0.0918. see C(3), again above 5%.

i. R-squared, an indication of the fit of your model. It lies between zero and 1 (or 0 and 100%), a value of zero or close to it means you explain just about nothing of the variantion in your dependent variable, so your model as a whole is rubbish. However, this does not mean your individual coefficients cannot be significant. There may still be a solid relation to be found amidst a sea of unexplained noise. Vice versa, you might have a high R-squared (origninal example on previous page) but with all or some (C(3,4)) coefficients which are not individually significant.

j. Adjusted R-squared. Same as R-squared, but with a correction so that it won't go up if you add a completely redundant variable to your model.

5. Tweaking to your regression, and testing if it works.

Often, your dataset needs to be tweaked in order to produce the best results - the results that contain the answers you need. As it is good practice to always keep the original data (even if we don't use all of it), this boils down to adding new variables; in EVIEWS this is known as adding a series. One reason to add a new series to your workfile is to see if it provides a better fit – in some circumstances a transformed variable can be a superior choice. We'll discuss several options and how to implement them, followed by a special case – Taylor's Theorem – which provides a very useful framework to capture non-linear relations in a (by necessity linear) regression , as well as the multicollinearity problem that often follows – and often occurs even without any adjustments. Finally, a test is discussed to see if all these additions do in fact improve your regression.

Generating new series

The first step is to decide what kind of transformation would be logical.

A. A logarithmic transformation.
B. Quadratic transformation
C. Prices and percentages
D. Categories

This decision should be based on the type of data you're using; a simple look at the spreadsheet view normally suffices.

A. Logarithmic transformation

If your data has a variable that moves over 3 orders of magnitude or more (so the smallest observation is more than 1000 times smaller than the largest), and these extremes aren't errors, then a *logarithmic transformation* is in order. Each observation should be replaced by it's log value, which indicates its order of magnitude. Log 10 = 1, log 100 = 2, log 1000 = 3, log 5000 = 3.69. Sometimes the 'natural logarithm' (ln, but sometime also 'log') is used, which produces different numbers (ln 2.718 = 1), but works equally well. EVIEWS follows this latter setup.

The reason for this transformation is that the residuals of your regression will generally have an order of magnitude that is at best one or two lower (so a factor of 10 to 100) than that of your observations. So if X is a large number, and your coefficient is off by even a little bit, your residual is likely to be large too. As OLS minimizes the sum of squared residuals, it would mean that the big observations are almost surely the ones driving the regressions results, ignoring the smaller ones. So you would treat your data on a vastly unequal footing.

An example would the population of a country (perhaps a proxy for the size of the market for certain goods). China and India would have values exceeding 1 billion (1.000.000.000), while Australia would be around 22 million (22.000.000). Say the residual associated with the former is 10%, so 100 million; the residual associated with Australia would need to be 450% to have the same impact. And squaring residuals will enlarge any differences; basically, Australia can produce whatever values it whishes, it wouldn't have any influence. Yet if we would take log values of the population variable, those for China and India would be around 9, while that for Australia would be 7.3. The result will be a regression that produces a much more accurate picture for all observations, instead of being skewed to the largest ones. NB: the 'three orders of magnitude' is a rule of thumb. With 2 orders (a factor 100) log transformations may sometimes be a good idea too, have a look at the errors in that case.

One caveat is that the logarithmic transformation doesn't apply to negative numbers. If you do have negative numbers (years with losses instead of profits, for example), it might be better to work with relative numbers (see subsection C), for example by taking the change relative to last year as a variable instead – thereby bringing all observations to a comparable scale. Further transformations to get rid of the negative values and then taking logarithms tend to make interpretation of the results quite hard.

B. Quadratic transformation

If you are more interested in changes in variables rather than absolute levels, a transformation to percentages is called for. The most common example of this is the use of returns, rather than prices in finance. If we want to compare two stocks, and the first changes from $125 to $130, that is a $5 profit, or 4%. The second stock changes from $1.00 to $1.50, or $0.50 in dollar terms, but 50%. If we'd have $10,000 to invest, the latter stock would have been vastly more profitable, but because of the different starting price, you can only reach this conclusion based on the percentage return, not on the dollar profit per share. This same problem occurs every time the basis for comparison differs between either observations (see the example regarding population above) or variables (the investment case).

In general, it is recommended that prices are transformed to returns, and if the dependent variable is a return, to transform as many of the independent variables as is logical – this makes the interpretation straightforward, and keeps the variables comparable (often within the same order of magnitude, even).

Last but not least, in many instances the changes are much more relevant than the levels, which are often arbitrary (reflecting structural market conditions). In most applications, one wants to know what is going to cause an adjustment of the status quo.

C. Prices and percentages

If your independent variables are non-numerical, but come in the form of categories (customers who return items vs. those who don't), dummies are needed. This technique is discussed in chapter 6.

D. Categories

If your data is expected to have a hill- or valley-shaped relation (so at first, when X goes up, so does Y, but Y will drop for higher values of X, or vice versa), a *quadratic transformation* is in order. This positive-relation-turning-negative often occurs when comparing production and profitability: a low production means relatively low profit due to start-up costs weighing more heavily, while a higher production means these costs can be spread over more units, increasing profits/unit. Yet at some point, adding capacity will be costly (e.g. overtime) which might decrease profits per unit.

The quadratic transformation simply involves taking the square of the independent variable, and adding this to the dataset. From there on, Talyor's theorem applies.

Taylor's Theorem

One of the downsides to quadratic transformations is that in practice, you seldom see relationships that closely follow such a pattern. In general, there is some sort of non-linear relation between X and Y variable, but the exact form remains to be seen. A useful tool to tackle this kind of situations is *Taylor's Theorem*. In essence it says that any non-linear relationship between X and Y can be captured using X, X^2, X^3, X^4 and so on as independent variables, *and* that this approximation gets better as more elements of this sequence ("higher order terms") are used. The only caveat is that you need a limited interval, but when applied to real-life data, which always has a beginning and an end (or highest and lowest value) that point is often moot. Figure 5.1 depicts the building blocks of the procedure; we can combine these to capture even very non-linear relations; Figure 5.2 offers an example. However, there are some downsides in including too many terms, as will be explained in the next section.

Figure 5.1

The basic shapes of a linear relation, a quadratic relation, and a cubed relation. Using Taylor's theorem, we can combine these to build a better fitting model.

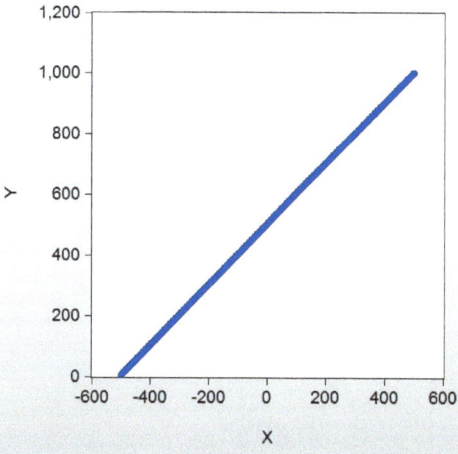

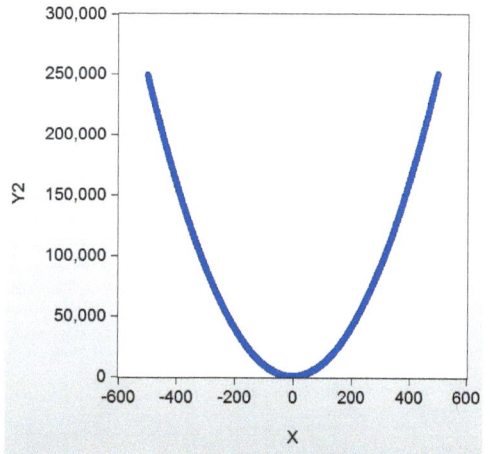

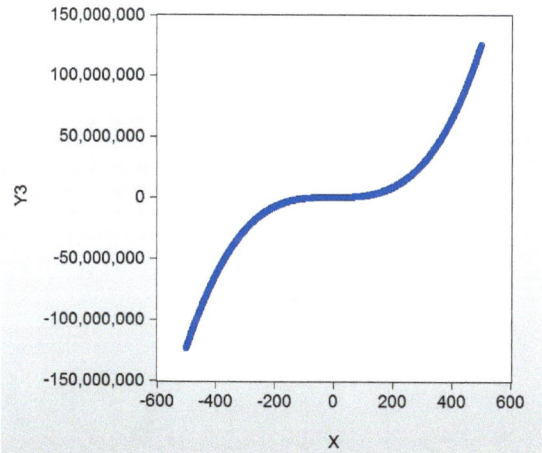

Figure 5.2

We have a very non-linear relation, and try a linear model (y=a+b*x+e), a second order approximation (y=a+b₁*x+b₂*x²+e), a third order (we add b₃*x³) as well as the 10th (which keeps adding terms up to and including x¹⁰). This last setup is very rarely used in practice; in this case there still is an improvement in fit, but the multicollinearity would not allow us to find any significant coefficients.

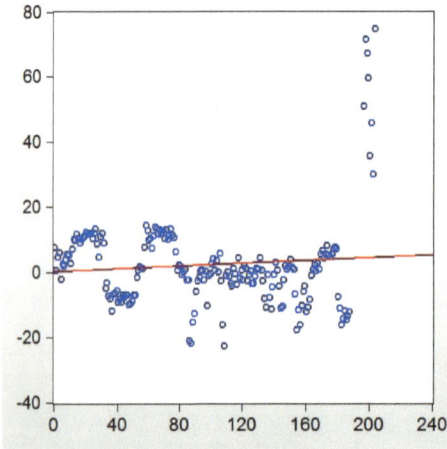

linear (first order)

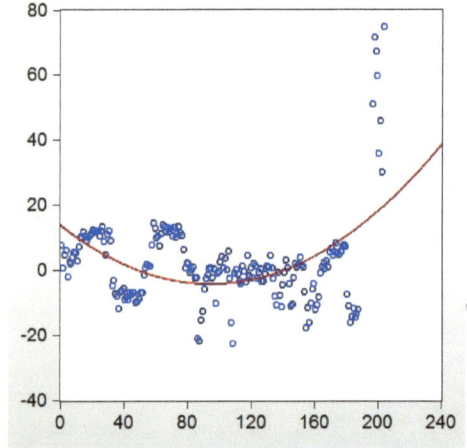

quadratic (second order)

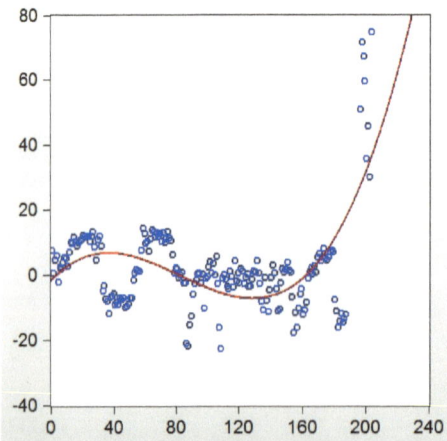

cubed (3rd order)

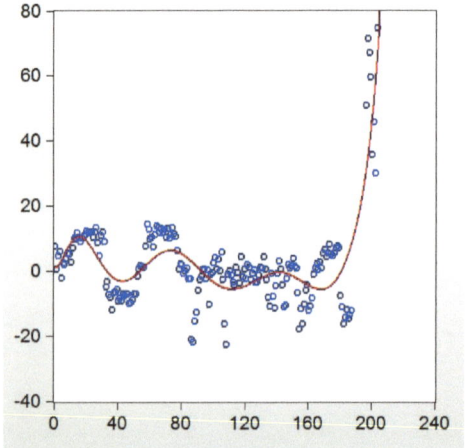

10th order

Multicollinearity

One problem that may arise out of using Taylor's theorem, is that of *multicollinearity*. This means that two or more of your independent variables are so alike, it's hard to reliably ascribe their effects on y to one variable or the other. In case of Taylor's theorem, it's easy to see that several variables will – at least over a certain interval – be similar, as they're based on the same underlying numbers.

In fact, this problem is much more general, as it can occur even with series that are not computed based on the same values.

The crucial element is that two independent variables cause comparable residuals. (The problem is therefore absent if you have just one independent variable). For this to happen, there has to be a linear relationship between X_1 and X_2. We can model that as follows:

$$X_{1,t} = c + dX_{2,t} + e$$

If this auxiliary regression has a good fit – a high R^2 – the independent variables will be similar. An example will illustrate the problem. We're estimating the following model:

$$y_t = a + b_1 X_{1t} + b_2 X_{2t} + e_t$$

Observation	Value for Y	Value for X_1	Value for X_2	Value for e based on a=0, b_1=1, b_2=2	Value for e based on a=0, b_1=0, b_2=4
t=1	5	2.5	1	0.5	1
t=2	-2	-1	-0.5	0	0
t=3	4.5	2	1	0.5	0.5
t=4	7.5	4	2	-0.5	-0.5
t=5	12	7	3	-1	0

In this example X_1 and X_2 are quite similar – the technical term is that they're highly correlated. This can be expressed in the form of a correlation coefficient (to be found in EVIEWS, under descriptive statistics of a group), but also in terms of the R^2 of a regression of X_1 on X_2. The consequences can also be seen fromt his table: in three out of the five cases shown, a model with the first set of coefficients (a=0, b_1=1, b_2=2) produces exactly the same residuals as the one with the second set of coefficients (a=0, b_1=0, b_2=4).

This means that in essence, we're down to two observations to determine which numbers correspond to the best set of coefficients. This arguably does not bode well for the reliability of our coefficients, in fact, we can derive an expanded formula for our standard errors:

$$S.E. = \sigma = \sqrt{\frac{\sigma_\varepsilon^2}{n\sigma_x^2(1 - R_{aux}^2)}}$$

This formula is the same as before, except for the addition of the R2 of the auxiliary regression – the one in the first equation on this page. It should be noted this equation only works for the case with two independent variables, but the mechanism is valid regardless of how many X-variables you have1. The more the (two) independent variables are correlated, the higher the R_{aux}^2 , and the higher our standard errors, making our coefficients less reliable! In fact, in many datasets this is the biggest driver of your standard errors, especially if market-based data is used. Due to increased integration of (especially) financial markets, shocks tend to show in all data-series, and thereby increase the correlation.

Should the R_{aux}^2 increase from 80% to 90% (0.8 to 0.9 in the formula), our standard errors double, as we divided by 0.2 beforehand, but by 0.1 afterwards, increasing the effect from a factor 5 to a factor 10.

If we follow this to its logical extreme, we even end up in a situation where we cannot estimate an OLS regression anymore; if you use two

---

[1] We would need matrix notation, which is a needless complication. The EVIEWS error message cited below is based on this notation.

independent variables that are identical after a linear transformation, the R^2_{aux} is 100%, we must divide by zero, which in essence produces infinite standard errors! So the model could be literally anything — clearly an unacceptable result. EVIEWS will act accordingly and produce an error message ('near singular matrix').

The more common term for this is *perfect multicollinearity*. It should be noted that it's often due to the analyst making a mistake, as no two real-life datasets tend to be *exactly* the same.

F-test

The test whether or not several additional variables are improving the model — that is, if they even belong in the model — is called the *F-test*. (Or, in EVIEWS, which uses a generalized version, the *Wald-test*).

The reason we need a new test is that the standard t-test will not suffice: if we test if a single coefficient differs from zero, we say nothing about the other coefficient(s) we want to involve in our test as well. This means that those other coefficients may adjust their values to compensate, as it were. If we want to test if two variables improve our model, we need to impose two restrictions at the same time — both coefficients need to be zero.

Of course, the same test is usable for other null-hypotheses, we can also test if $c(3)=7$ and $c(4)=-2$ if we'd want to. Which null-hypothesis is relevant depends on the type of info you want to get out of your analysis; perhaps an investment is only acceptable if the initial outlay (would could be modeled as the intercept) isn't bigger than 5 million and the profit per unit (a slope) is at least 20. The null-hypotheses that set coefficients equal to zero is used so often because this is the one that asks whether your variables should be in the model to begin with (see chapter 8), but it's not the only possibility.

The F-test works by checking the change in fit, as measured by the R^2: we compare the R^2 of an unrestricted model (the coefficients can be any value) with the restricted model where the coefficients assume the values dictated by the null-hypothesis. If the difference in R^2 is big enough, the restrictions imposed by the null hypothesis worsen the model, and the null hypothesis is rejected; this situation arises when the probability-value of the null being true is less than 5% (our significance level). On the other hand, if the two models perform roughly equally well, the null is not rejected.

However, the difference in R^2 cannot be directly used to produce a probability, we need to standardize this difference, taking the number of restrictions, the number of observations, the number of coefficients and the overall fit into account. This leads to the following formula:

$$F = \frac{(R^2_{unrestr.model} - R^2_{restricted\ model})/(number\ of\ restrictions)}{(1 - R^2_{unrestr.model})/(obs. - number\ of\ indep.variables - 1)}$$

This F-statistic follows a so-called F-distribution, which makes it possible to put a p-value on it. (The degrees of freedom, needed to find the right place in a table if one would use that method rather than relying on EVIEWS, are equal to the number of restrictions for the numerator, and the number of observations minus the number of independent variables minus 1 for the denominator, just as in the formula above) .

The F-test is an important tool in arriving at the correct *specification* - i.e., finding out which variables should be included in the model (see chapter 8).

Webcasts

Relevant webcasts for this chapter are:

5. The F-test

6. Transforming data

6. Dummies

We often encounter the situation where our data does not come in the form of a numerical variable, but is divided in categories (for example: small, medium and large businesses, or the American, European and Asian divisions, or corporate versus private clients, etc.). If we have such data as our dependent variable, OLS would not be helpful, and we'd have to switch to a (multinominal) logit model, which is outside the scope of this book. However, most of the time categorical data are independent variables, and OLS *can* use these as inputs – after a bit of tweaking.

The necessary transformation is achieved by creating so-called *dummy-variables*. These have only two possible values, either 0 or 1. (Even if we have more than two categories, this binary setup will work, as explained below, but for now assume just two categories). This allows us differentiate between the situation where the extra variable is 'turned on' – the dummy has a value of 1 - and 'turned off' – the dummy has a value of 0. It might seem such a transformation embodies little progress, but if we switch to equations, and realize that to multiply something by zero always results in an outcome of zero, progress comes rapidly:

$Y = a + b_1 * X_1 + b_2 * dummy * X_1 + e$

If we assign the value of zero to the dummy for all our corporate clients, the equation becomes $Y = a + b_1 * X_1 + e$ for them, but for the private clients, where the value of the dummy equals one, we can re-write the equation as $Y = a + (b_1 + b_2) * X_1 + e$. The difference is that the private client can now have a different slope coefficient! Note that b_2 can be both positive and negative, so the slope can be either steeper or flatter. And because all observations for corporate clients result in multiplications with zero, b_2 is estimated solely using the private clients, so that b1 represents the slope for the corporate ones, and the sum of $b_1 + b_2$ the private ones, separating the two classes.

Of course, the intercept is in this setup equal for both categories. This may be appropriate, but it is possible that the intercept differs too. In that case we need to expand the model a bit, and apply the dummy variable also to the intercept:

$Y = a_1 + a_2 * dummy + b_1 * X_1 + b_2 * dummy * X_1 + e$

This translates to the following setup: for corporate clients (dummy = 0) the equation is:

$Y = a_1 + b_1 * X_1 + e$

Which we can interpret in the usual way. But for the private clients (dummy = 1) we have:

$Y = (a_1 + a_2) + (b_1 + b_2) * X_1 + e$

This means that our intercept and slope can change between the categories; a_2 and b_2 are dummy *coefficients*. Figure 6.1 gives some graphical examples.

Figure 6.1

Suppose we have the following equation: Size_portfolio = c(1) + c(2)*dummy + c(3)*market + c(4) * dummy * market. This would be the EVIEWS-equivalent of Y = a₁ + a₂ * dummy + b₁ *X + b2 * dummy *X + e applied to the problem we studied earlier.

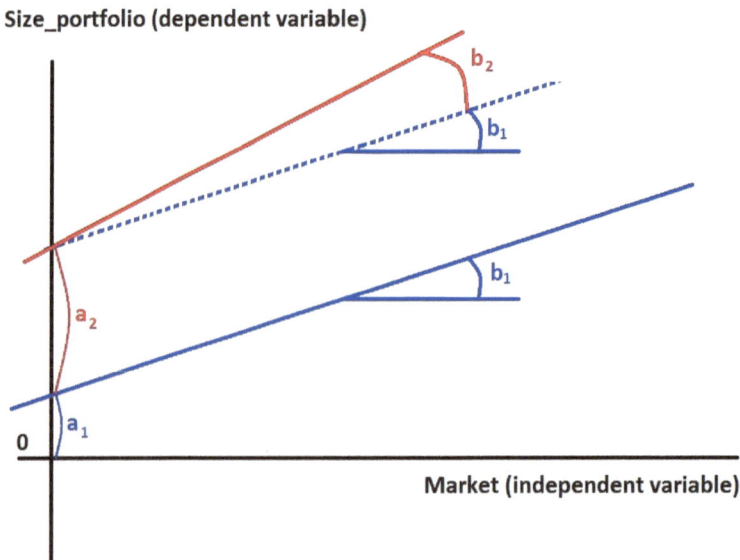

Size_portfolio (dependent variable)

b_2

b_1

b_1

a_2

0 a_1

Market (independent variable)

And if we allow the intercept and all slopes to differ between categories, our results will be the same as if we'd run a separate regression for each category. However, since the difference is embodied in the dummy-coefficients, *we can also asses the reliability of the differences*; something that's impossible with different regressions.

And if we want to know if this division into two categories is supported by the data, we can resort to testing if the dummy-coefficients (a_2 and b_2 in our example) are significantly different from zero. If we only have an intercept to test, or a single slope, a t-test will do. If we have both an intercept- and slope-coefficient – as in Figure 6.1 – we need an F-test with null-hypothesis that $a_2 = 0$ and $b_2 = 0$.

Three or more categories

In case we have three or more categories, a slight modification is needed. Since we still would like to isolate each category, we need multiple dummy variables. In fact, if we have k categories, we need k-1 dummies; the first one – called the *base case* – can simply be covered by setting all other dummies to zero. Table 6.1 gives an overview of how one should construct the dummy-variables, if category A is the base case. Should we want another category as the base-case, then we have to define the dummy-variables in such a way they are all zero for that particular category.

The equation then becomes:

$Y = a_1 + a_2 *$ dummy$_1 + a_3 *$ dummy$_2 + b_1 * X_1 + b_2 *$ dummy$_1 * X_1 + b_3 *$ dummy$_2 * X_1 + e$

Because we have an additional category, we need an additional dummy variable; apart from the first two categories we covered before, we now also need to know if category 3 (represented by dummy 2!) is 'on' or 'off' (1 or 0).

Table 6.1

Observation	category	Value for dummy$_1$	Value for dummy$_2$	Value for dummy$_3$	Value for dummy$_4$
t=1	A	0	0	0	0
t=2	B	1	0	0	0
t=3	C	0	1	0	0
t=4	D	0	0	1	0
t=5	E	0	0	0	1
t=6	C	0	1	0	0
t=7	A	0	0	0	0
t=8	B	1	0	0	0
t=9	B	1	0	0	0
t=10	E	0	0	0	1
t=11	D	0	0	1	0
t=12	C	0	1	0	0

Levels- and changes specifications.

Thus far, we've employed what's called a *changes-specification*. An alternative way of using dummy-variables is the so-called *levels-specification*. This setup doesn't emphasize the changes relative to a base-case, but treats all categories equally, and is focused on the extent the coefficients differ from zero.

With a levels-specification, two adjustments need to be made : we need a dummy variable for each category, as there is no base-case, and secondly, we need to drop the regular constant / slope variable (again, because that reflected the base-case, which is not relevant in the levels-specification). We'll use the example with small, medium and large enterprises, which now needs 3 dummies, see table 6.2:

Table 6.2

Observation	category	Value for dum S	Value for dumM	Value for dum L
t=1	Medium	0	1	0
t=2	Small	1	0	0
t=3	Medium	0	1	0
t=4	Large	0	0	1
t=5	Large	0	0	1

The equation then becomes:

$$Y = a_1*dumS + a_2*dumM + a_3*dumL + b_1*dumS *x+ b_2*dumM*X + b_3*dumL* X + e$$

The coefficients a_1, a_2 and a_3 now denote the intercept for Small, Medium and Large companies, b_1 to b_3 their slopes.

Often, the question arises if you should use a levels- or changes-specification. The answer simply depends on which standard errors you need. The coefficients themselves can be recalculated: the slope in the changes specification (for a category with dummy =1) is b_1 +b_2, while in the levels specification it's just b_2. So the same information with respect to the coefficients is present in either setup. Yet standard errors can't be added, so if you want to know the standard error for the slope for category B, you *need* a levels-specification, if you want to test if the difference is significant, you *need* a changes specification.

Practical issues:

- It's rarely a good idea to use slope-dummies without an intercept dummy. If a single constant has to apply to all observations, you force both models to go through the same point – namely the intersection with the vertical axis. This may cause substantial distortions, as the picture below shows.

Figure 6.2

The blue dots represent observations from one group, the black dots from another; the lines of those respective colors the relations we should get - and will gte with both intercept and slope dummies. The red lines represent the models that have an identical intercept (so no intercept dummy is present). We see that neither of the red lines is a good representation of the data; errors in the intercept will also affect the slope-coefficients.

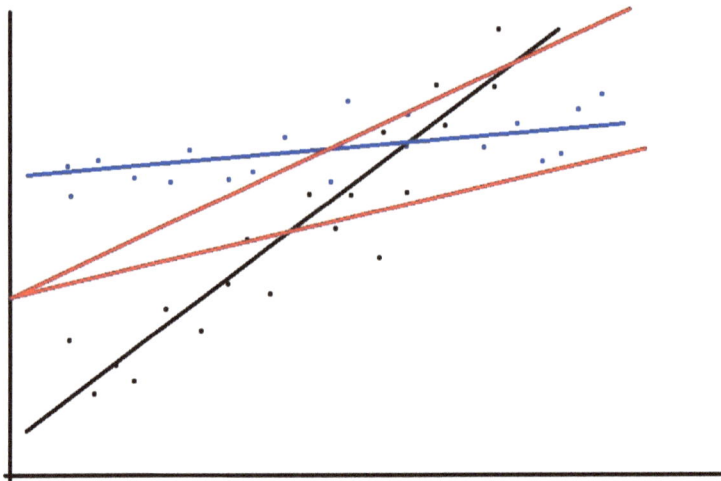

- In many cases it may not be directly obvious which category should act as the base-case. If you're only interested in the coefficients, this would not matter, as we can easily calculate those relative to any choice of a base-case. For the standard errors this cannot be done however; the standard error of the sum of two coefficients cannot be reconstructed from the original standard errors. The only solution to this problem is to re-estimate the model with a different base case or as a levels-specification.

Webcasts

Through www.covariance.nl you can find a series of webcasts that will help you with EVIEWS. The relevant webcast for this chapter is:

9. Dummies

Part III : Anything that can go wrong...

Now we've established how to estimate a regression and which factors drive its results, we need to have a closer look into the problems that may arise. Data analysis obeys Murphy's Law: anything that can go wrong, will go wrong - eventually. We'll see that OLS will give us good quality results under a specific set of circumstances only. If those circumstances – more formally, assumptions – do not apply, we have many tools to fix the problems, but in order to arrive at a remedy we first need to establish what those assumptions are, the consequences of them being violated as well as how this will occur in practice, and how we can detect those violations. Then, and only then, can we discuss the remedies.

It should be noted that the next chapters focus on methodological problems; we're looking at situations where OLS fails to give good quality answers because *the OLS method* isn't capable of dealing with the type of problem we face – at least not without some corrections.[2] Methodological problems are rooted in a violation of the basic assumptions underlying OLS.

Basic assumptions

The list of assumptions under which OLS is BLUE won't be proven, but just given:

---

[2] OLS may also fail to give good quality answers even if all assumptions are met and the method is just fine, simply because the data doesn't allow for anything better. (For example, your standard errors can be too big to reach any meaningful conclusions because of a small sample size). Those issues – and possible solutions – were discussed in chapter 4.

Table 7.1

Basic assumptions of OLS

Assumption I: the model is correctly specified.
This includes: no omitted variables, no duplicate variables, and residuals which are zero on average. See chapter 8.
Assumption II: each observation contains the same amount of information.
This combines two conditions, both related to the residuals: they must have a constant variance (homoskedasticity) and there must be no (serial) correlation between them. Since OLS treats every residual in the same way, a situation where some observations are much more reliable than others or where residuals can predict each other, will distort your results. See chapter 9.
Assumption III: there's no distortion in the independent variables
This means that X much not be influenced by Y as well (which would create a chicken-and-egg question, technically known as endogeneity), and X must not be subject to random (measurement) errors. See chapter 10.

These assumptions underlying OLS are a result of the *Gauss-Markov Theorem*. This theorem establishes that under the assumptions mentioned above, OLS will be *BLUE* – the Best Linear Unbiased Estimator. These terms each have a specific meaning:

- 'Best' means that the estimation procedure produces the lowest possible standard errors. Our results are therefore the most reliable ones we can get (but also see the next term).

- Linear means the relation between dependent (Y) and independent (X) variables is linear; the guarantee of 'best' only applies to comparisons with linear models. This doesn't rule out the use of Taylor's Theorem to capture non-linearity though (see chapter 4), but it does preclude multiplicative interactions, such as $Y = a+bX_1X_2+e$.

- *Unbiased* means that our results are *on average* right. If we would repeat OLS numerous times with different datasets that all follow the same underlying relation between X and Y, we would a set of coefficients for each regression. The average of those coefficients would be the correct value. Technically, the assumption says the expectation is equal to the true value, but since the expectation in mathematical terms *is nothing else than the average*, we tend to formulate it as we did above.

- Estimator means that we're analyzing an estimation procedure, in this case OLS.

The Gauss-Markov theorem establishes the desirable properties of OLS if the assumptions are met. Deviations for this ideal are frequent, and will be discussed in the next chapters. In other to assess the consequences of those violations, we need to discuss three concepts: bias, efficiency and consistency.

7. Bias, Efficiency and consistency

If we have a problem when analyzing data through regression analysis - and one would be very lucky to have real-life datasets that don't throw at least one or two of these problems your way - we can study the consequences through three concepts: *Bias*, *Efficiency* and *Consistency*. Only once we know what the consequences of a problem are, will we be able to find the best solution to the problem, as in many cases we'll have to weigh various alternatives that each have their own flaws.

Bias

Bias is the opposite of unbiased, as discussed above: if we have bias, are results are, on average, *wrong*. A biased coefficient or standard error cannot be relied upon. There is always some uncertainty regarding the correct numbers, but in case of a biased number this uncertainty is centered around the wrong value. Even on average we will not find the correct numbers, and it is very likely that our estimates will be too high much more often than too low, or vice versa. Figure 7.1 illustrates this.

Figure 7.1

The horizontal axis shows the coefficient we find with OLS and the true value; the difference is the bias. The vertical axis shows the probability of finding a coefficient of that value; with a bias the chances of finding the right value decrease substantially, and deviations may be much larger than expected, as the probabilities are highest around the biased value.

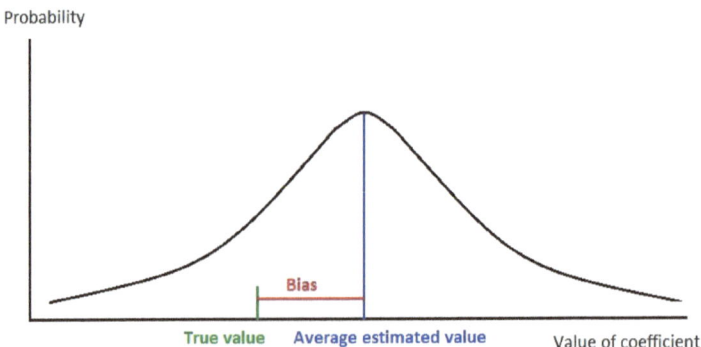

NB: It should be noted that bias can apply to the coefficients of a regression (as show in Figure 7.1), but also to its standard errors.

Efficiency

Efficiency is the degree to which the estimation procedure uses the available information to produce reliable coefficients. An efficient estimation procedure will therefore have the lowest possible standard errors; those indicate reliability. An inefficient procedure has higher standard errors, which may ultimately remove the ability to reject any relevant null-hypothesis. In that case, no conclusions can be drawn from the data since no possibility can be ruled out.

Figure 7.2

The horizontal axis shows the coefficient we find with OLS (which we assume here is equal to the true value). The vertical axis shows the probability of finding a coefficient of that value; with a bigger standard error the probability of finding values which are further away from the average is clearly bigger. Estimation method A is more efficient.

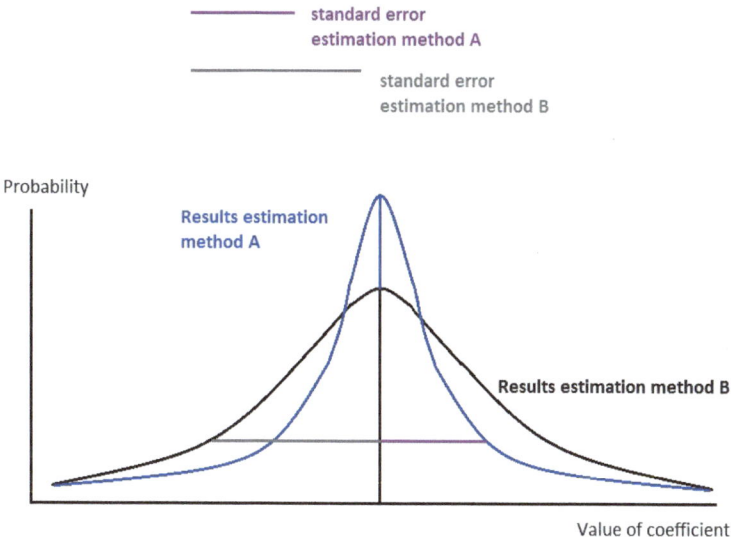

standard error estimation method A

standard error estimation method B

Probability

Results estimation method A

Results estimation method B

Value of coefficient

Often efficiency is analyzed together with bias; there are many cases where bias can be reduced at the cost of efficiency. Figure 7.3 illustrates this by showing two models, one with a bias but low standard errors, another without any bias but with high standard errors.

Figure 7.3.

The horizontal axis shows the coefficients we may find with either model; the vertical axis shows the probability of finding a coefficient of that value. Model A produces an unbiased estimate, but with high uncertainty, while model B will be on average wrong (by a fairly small amount, the bias) but is unlikely to produce estimates far removed from its average (low standard errors).

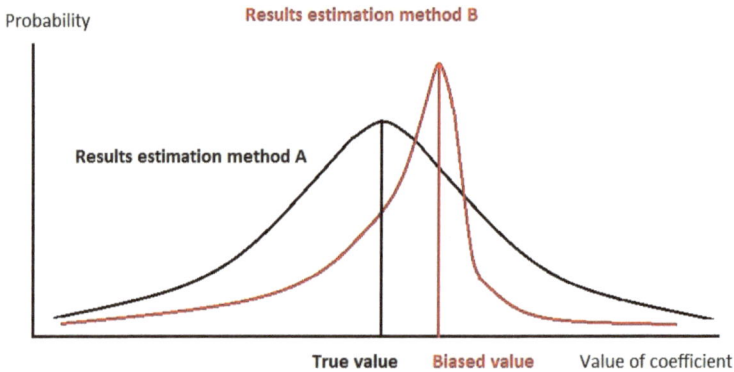

In many cases, model B in Figure 7.3 would in fact be better than model A, as the chance of finding a coefficient that's closer to the mark is a lot higher, even though we have some bias. Chapter 8 explores this trade-off in the context of omitted (missing) variables in your model.

Consistency

Consistency is a feature of a good model, it's defined as follows: a consistent estimator is one that produces the exact right number (without standard error) for our coefficients if we would have a dataset of infinite size. Of course, a dataset of infinite size is a theoretical construct, but a consistent estimator will produce better estimates as the sample size get larger. So our results become more reliable if we get more data. As increasing the amount of data is the number one tool to improve your results, consistency is a much desired feature. If it's absent – the estimator is inconsistent – we have a serious problem, since this must mean that our estimate is biased, and this bias will not disappear if we add more data, leaving us with fewer options to improve our results.

Figure 7.4 illustrates the difference between a consistent estimation procedure and an inconsistent one. For the sake of clarity, we assume that beyond a certain level, the bias is unacceptable.

Figure 7.4

The number of observations plotted against bias. The inconsistent estimator has a bias that is not responding to the number of observations (so the bias will be there even in an infinitely sized dataset). If this bias is unacceptably large, as it is here, we're out of luck: the estimation procedure is useless. A consistent estimator, represented by the curve, will eventually eliminate its bias, so regardless of where the threshold between acceptable and unacceptable bias lies, you can always get below it by adding more data.

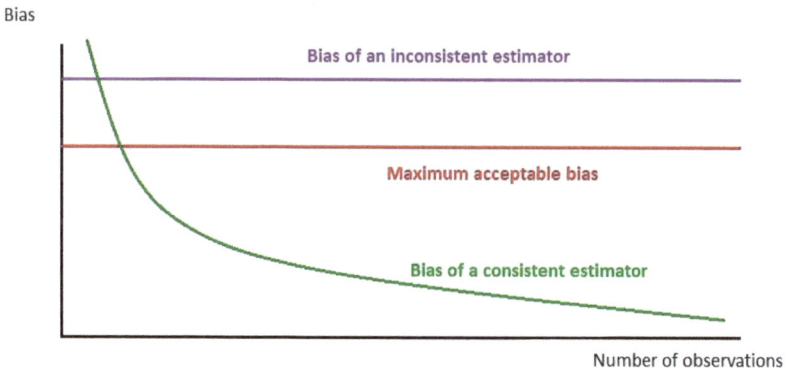

Bias

Bias of an inconsistent estimator

Maximum acceptable bias

Bias of a consistent estimator

Number of observations

Part IV : ..... should be fixed!

Any of the assumptions may be violated in practice, and any such violation causes a deterioration in the quality of the results. The key to have a good analysis is therefore to minimize such violations. While this ideal isn't fully attainable (it's impossible to know for certain your model is absolutely correct in its specification), reducing errors and uncertainty can go a long way indeed.

The next chapters will discuss each assumption, following the same setup; we'll define the problem, give example of how the problem is likely to arise in real-life data, discuss the consequences, how to detect the problem (diagnosis) and how to remedy it. When discussing consequences, we'll do so in terms of bias, efficiency and consistency of the coefficients, possible bias in the standard errors, and the effect on the goodness-of-fit (the R^2 of the model). Every segment ends with a table that gives a concise overview; the reader is strongly encouraged to produce his own version of this on a single piece of paper, adding his or her own notes; such an overview has been proven to be invaluable as a study-tool, but only if you make it yourself and add your own comments.

8. Omitted and redundant variables

The first problem with regression analysis arises before we even boot the computer: we have to come up with a model that has the right specification. This means that there are neither too few nor too many variables in the equation, and that all variables are transformed in such a way they fit a single, linear relation.

Those last bits may require some clarification. As for the 'single relation': it is perfectly possible that the relation between dependent and independent variable(s) changes halfway through your dataset. Maybe a new major competitor entered the market, maybe a company's profile changed due to mergers or acquisitions, or maybe the regulatory or political situation changed. Luckily we already discussed a way of dealing with this: dummy variables. If we identify the structural break – the place where the relation shifted – we can simply regard 'before' and 'after' as different categories, and create a dummy that assigns the value 0 to the first situation, and 1 to the second. Additional bonus is that we can immediately see if that distinction was necessary to begin with (i.e., if the dummy coefficients are significantly different from zero).

As for the second condition, the linearity of the relation between X and Y is a cornerstone of regression analysis. However, this may be too much of an abstraction: many relationships in empirical data are non-linear. Panel C and D of Figure 2.1 give some examples. In such a case, a Taylor approximation can be helpful, sometimes other transformations are required (see chapter 5).

But all this doesn't rule out the most common form of this problem: if I want to find out if my advertisement efforts improved sales, do I need to include the advertisement spending of competitors in the regression too? After all, it is a potentially relevant piece of data.

The answer, in general, would be *yes*. Leaving a relevant variable out of your regression will have more severely negative consequences than including a redundant variable. Moreover, we'll only be able to tell if a variable is indeed redundant untill we've included it, and finally, nothing is easier than throwing out a redundant variable.

But the other side of the coin is that, in most applications, we'll lack data on one or more variables that we believe might be relevant, and that for the sake of giving the complete picture, it's sometimes necessary to keep superfluous variables in the model. It therefore pays to study the effects of both omitted and redundant variables.

Omitted variables

a. Definition of the problem, example

An omitted variable means that a variable that should be in the model (because it significantly contributes to explaining the dependent variable) is left out. For all intents and purposes, this means that while we should have a non-zero slope coefficient, we force the model by design to have a coefficient of zero, eliminating the influence of this variable – multiplying it by zero gives a zero for each observation. A day-to-day example would be ignore whether one's travelling uphill or downhill when measuring the fuel-efficiency of your car; a more business-related one would be to ignore age or disposable income when predicting how much consumers will buy, or market conditions in a business-to-business context.

b. Consequences

Omitted variables tend to influence your coefficient estimates, your standard errors and the goodness-of-fit (R^2) of your model.

Impact on coefficients

The consequences of an omitted variable depend on how strong the omitted variable is related to those variables that *are* included in the regression. The reason for this is that, if there exists a relation between included and excluded variables, some of the influence which should be ascribed to the omitted variable *is transferred to the variables that are still included in the model*.

In other words: if variable z has an influence but is not in the model, but doubling the coefficient of variable x will capture part of this effect because x and z are very much alike, OLS will do that, as this will reduce the residuals. The coefficients of included variables therefore will contain some effects due to omitted variables, and because of that, the coefficients will have the wrong values – they're biased. This *Omitted Variable Bias* is the main consequence, and it affects all variables that are still in the model, unless they're completely independent of the omitted variable. That exception is extremely rare in practice, though it would mean that an omitted variable would have no consequences at all, except for a lower R^2.

Let's illustrate the effects by using three regressions: the first one has just one independent variable

1) $y_j = a_1 + b_1 x_j + \varepsilon_{1j}$ $\quad J = 1,...,n$

Now this looks like a perfectly fine regression model, with intercept a_1, slope-coefficient b_1, a residual series and n observations, indicated by the subscript j. But suppose we use the equation above while the proper model – one that doesn't omit variables – is the one below:

2) $y_j = a_2 + b_2 x_j + c_2 z_j + \varepsilon_{2j}$ $\quad J = 1,...,n$

We have an additional independent variable, called z (in this case, using X_2 as a symbol would probably be confusing). It was omitted in the first model. Using the first equation instead of the second one has consequences, which can be shown using an *auxiliary regression* where we study how much of the omitted variable z is related to the included variable x.

3) $z_j = a_3 + b_3 x_j + \varepsilon_{3j}$ $J = 1,....,n$

If this auxiliary regression has an R^2 bigger than zero, x and z are correlated. This means that in model 1 – the one we mistakenly use – part of the effect of z can end up in the coefficient for x. After all, while OLS cannot reduce the residuals using a variable that's not in the model, it can increase the coefficient of a variable that is present. The problem is that by doing this, the effect of x seems bigger than it really is, since part of the slope coefficient is due to z, not x. This difference is a *bias* in the slope coefficient. The more x can replace the effects of z, the bigger this bias in coefficient b_1. We can even calculate how big this bias is:

$$Coefficient = b_2 + c_1 b_3$$

The coefficient is equal to the true value (b_2) plus c_1 multiplied by b_3. This product $c_1 b_3$ is therefore the bias, as an unbiased estimate has to be correct on average.

Conclusion from this piece of maths: we'll always have an omitted variable bias, unless:
- the omitted variables aren't significant ($c_1 = 0$), or
- the omitted variable is not related to the included variable(s); this means $b_3 = 0$.

Impact on standard errors
The effect on the standard errors is harder to pinpoint exactly; the reason for this is that when coefficient change, the residuals change with them, and that influences the standard errors. On the other hand, one effect is clear: if we omit a variable that is correlated with other included variables, we'll have reduced the amount of multicollinearity in the model. This would actually improve (lower) the standard errors of the remaining coefficients, which is a good thing.
This means that sometimes, omitting a variable can also be a conscious decision in the trade-off between bias and efficiency. Omitting a variable causes bias, but perhaps this bias is small (for example, due to a low c1 coefficient in the example above) and the gains in terms of

efficiency – lower standard errors – are enough to prioritize this effect over the bias. Also see Figure 7.3.

Impact on R^2

Leaving out a relevant variable will always decrease the R^2 – in fact, the definition of a relevant variable is that it significantly increases the performance of your model (also see the section on the F-test).

c. Diagnosis

A diagnostic test for omitted variables faces the problem that one doesn't know the nature of the omitted variable, unless one has a variable – and data for that variable – in which case you can simply add the variable and test for redundancy. This can be done using the by now familiar t-test (for a single variable) or F-test (if we test for redundancy of multiple variables).

Diagnosis therefore requires that we have data on the variable that is supposedly missing. This means it is a good idea to collect data on any variable that might conceivably have an impact, even if your main research question does not involve those variables. Candidates for omitted variables will differ for each field and purpose, so experience – and use of earlier research – will be valuable. In the most general terms, you have to ask yourself "Are all my observations pretty much the same, and if not, in which ways are they different? Could those differences perhaps have an impact on the observations / their behavior?" For example, if each observation represents a person, it's common to check for age as an omitted variable, as that influences many types of behavior. Note that often, we include variables that we're not strictly speaking interested in (in terms of answering the question we want answered). These so-called *control variables* are purely added to diagnose and fix omitted variable bias.

In some cases - if one suspects structural breaks or non-linear elements – the variable that needs to be added requires some work and/or an experienced eye. These two problems can often be spotted from the residual plot: if the residuals suddenly follow a different pattern (for example, change from largely positive to largely negative, or have much bigger values; see illustrations below), this is an indication of a *structural break* – a change in the parameters that indicates we've omitted a necessary dummy variable.

Again, to diagnose this, we need to include the supposedly omitted variable, and test for redundancy. In this case, the omitted variable would be a dummy, with a value of zero before the break and 1 afterwards (or vice versa).

Figure 8.1

Residual plot: the model performs much worse after 2002, suggesting a structural break. The omitted variable is a dummy (in combination with another slope variable, which may or may not already be present in the model)

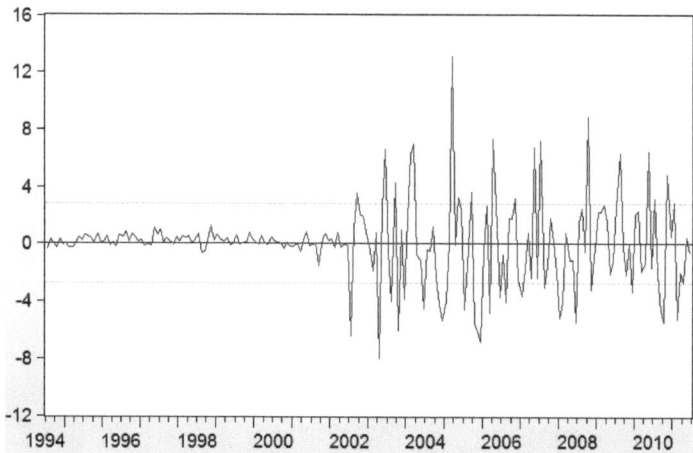

NB: this figure is also an example of heteroskedasticity (see chapter 9)

If there is a non-linear relation, Taylor's theorem (see chapter 5) should be used; first construct squared versions of the data, then test. Be especially careful for multicollinearity though if you also use higher orders. The figure below gives an example of the relation and residual plot that you could expect in such a case (before adding the omitted higher order terms). Note that residuals are above or below their average value of zero for many observations in a row.

Figure 8.2

Top: a non-linear relation; X on the horizontal axis, Y on the vertical. Bottom: the resulting residuals if we would use just a linear model (vertical axis).NB: the horizontal axis in the bottom panel shows the number of the observation.

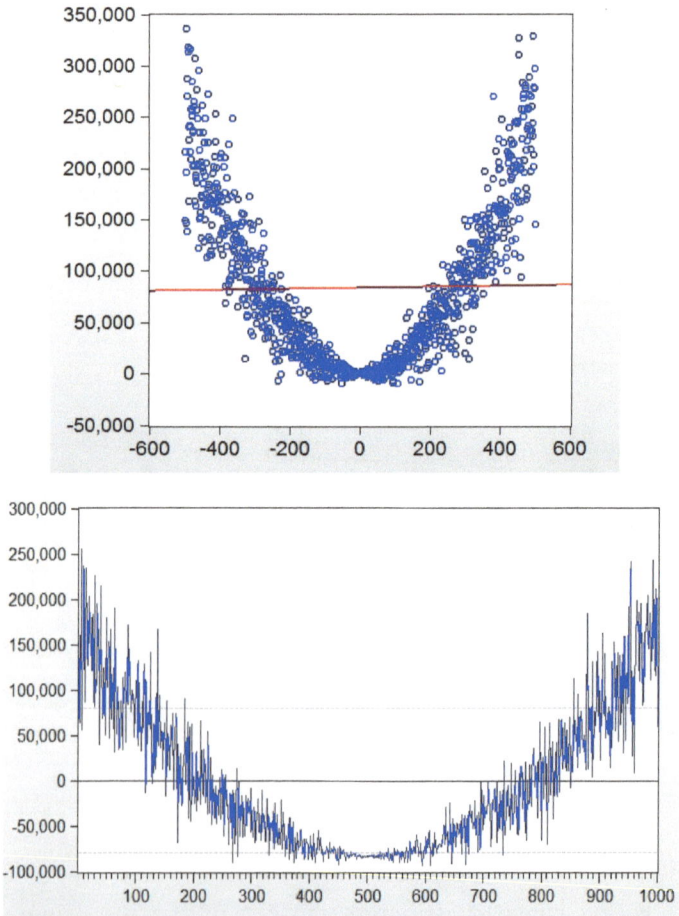

d. Remedy

The only proper fix to an omitted variable problem is to get the data, include it in the regression, and work with the new results. If the data is available, or can be obtained – perhaps after a transformation – the remedy is already included in the diagnosis. (For the remedy when the omitted variable is a non-linear term, see chapter 5, for the situation where it is categorical data (i.e., non-numerical), see chapter 6)

But getting data on an omitted variable can be tricky; the data may be unavailable altogether or of poor quality. In the first case one can either accept this state of affairs, or search for a variable that approximates the one we really need. Such a proxy variable is likely to result in poor quality data as well; we then should balance the possible bias due to errors-in-variables (see chapter 10) with the omitted variable bias. The magnitude of the omitted variable bias is determined by the correlation between included and excluded variables, and often someone with experience (regarding the data we're analyzing) will be able to give at least a rough estimate.

For example, if the advertisement efforts of the competition is an omitted variable, one should consider if in this market it is common to respond to the competition, wait till the storm has passed for launching one's own efforts (which are *both* likely to cause a more profound correlation, in one case we advertise when the others do as well – positive correlation; in the other when we don't – negative correlation) or ignore others altogether (low or no correlation).

One could say that if this correlation is low, and the errors-in-variables are high, it would be best to disregard the omitted variable problem; but if the situation is reversed, this would be a very bad idea. It should be noted though that a precise estimate of the two biases will often be impossible (we'd need accurate data for that, and its absence is the root of the problem); there's no substitute for experience in these matters, as in the end one has to make a judgment call.

e. Overview: omitted variable

Assumption	**All relevant variables are included in the model**
Definition	No variables are missing, categorical data has appropriate dummies, non-linearities are linearized.
Example violation	Virtually all financial data, where we want to explain returns; actions of the competition
Consequences	Bias in your coefficients; magnitude depends on the correlation between omitted and included variables. Because of this: standard errors and R^2 also biased.
Diagnosis	Include a candidate for an omitted variable, and test if it's significant
Remedy	Adjust your regression model

Practical issues:

- When there are a great many variables that could potentially be relevant in your model, it may be best to first see if among all these variable there are perhaps pairs that are closely correlated (for example, French and German bond yields in 2002-2011). If so, it's more convenient to look at just a single one.
- Introducing new variables may in fact lead to higher standard errors on the coefficients of existing variables, due to multicollinearity. It may also change the coefficients themselves due to the removal of omitted variable bias, even affecting their sign (positive or negative). This may trigger a lot of adjustments back-and-forth (also see the

next section); if that occurs err on the side of caution and reduce the omitted variable bias.

- Accepting a bit of bias for an efficiency gain is sometimes a good choice (Figure 7.3 illustrates this). A tool for this decision is the *Mean-Squared Error criterion*: take the square of the bias, and add to that number the variance of the coefficient (the square of the standard error). The model for which this number is lowest is often regarded as the best.
- But even if the MSE improves, keep in mind that having biased results can be a hard sale to some audiences; prepare to explain *why* you made this choice. Also, if your standard errors are low already (coefficients related to your research question are significant), or inconsequential (the variables will clearly never be significant) it's not worth it to risk a bias for a change in standard errors.
- If we omit the intercept in a model, rather than an independent variable, we run the risk of biasing our results in a similar way as in Figure 6.2, as we'd force the regression line to go through the origin (the intersection of the axis, the point 0,0) while it probably shouldn't go through that point at all. This will cause a violation of the assumption that your residuals are zero on average. (and sometimes this is listed as a separate assumption of the Gauss-Markov framework)

Redundant variables

a. Definition of the problem, example

A *redundant variable* simply means that we put a variable in the model that has no function there. It doesn't explain anything (therefore the slope coefficient for this variable will be zero, or not significantly different for zero, see below). A redundant variable is just dead weight in a regression. Then why would we include it? The reason is that you normally don't know that a variable is redundant till you put it in the model and estimate that model. So many candidate variables for an omitted variable end up being redundant. Suppose you want to estimate ice cream sales based on the temperature and the amount of wind. If the wind doesn't influence the sales (for example, because people go to your beach-front vendor anyway), it's a redundant variable.

b. Consequences

A purely redundant variable has only one consequence: standard errors of all coefficients for variables correlated to the redundant variable are increased. In other words: we'll have more multicollinearity (see chapter X). A truly redundant variable will have a slope-coefficient of zero, and therefore no impact on the residuals and therefore no impact on the R^2 of the regression. However, there's some difference between the theory above and practice.

In practice we might see some change in the numbers, as the slope coefficient is always an estimate. This estimate may deviate a bit from zero; by definition the (slope-) coefficient of a redundant variable is insignificant, but that means we cannot *determine* if it's different from zero, not that it is exactly zero. So a number that is unequal to zero is possible, as long as it's small relative to the standard error. Using real data, we therefore will regularly see that a redundant variable has small effects on other coefficients and the R^2. These effects could be in either direction, again by definition, they would be small enough to be insignificant, and therefore should be ignored.

The effect on the standard errors, in contrast, can be profound, both in theory and practice. Suppose that we want to explain the price of copper, initially using two variables: global GDP (X_1) and electricity consumption (X_2). Now assume that a third variable is added, which is a development index (X_3), calculated by taking (with a 50% weight) GDP developments, and electricity consumption (also 50%)! Lastly, assume that this development index also contains some noise, otherwise we'd have perfect multicollinearity (see chapter 6), and couldn't even estimate this model. Clearly, even with the noise, the third variable (or one of the two original ones, that doesn't matter) is redundant; $2X_1+3X_2 = X_1+2X_2+2X_3$, except for the bit of noise. In fact, X_2+2X_3 (so without X_1) gives us the same number. Our coefficients are therefore highly uncertain, and the standard errors reflect this: as the noise becomes smaller, the standard errors increase – eventually to infinity!

c. Diagnosis

In the case of a single redundant variable, a diagnostic test is simple: a t-test will suffice. If the probability (p-value) is above 5%, you cannot reject the null-hypothesis that the slope coefficient is zero, so you cannot reject the variable is redundant – so it *is* redundant.

It becomes a bit more involved if we're dealing with multiple variables that may all be redundant. It is quite possible that you have a set of variables that are all insignificant individually, but are jointly significant (this is the conclusion you reach if you conduct an F-test with the null that all slope-coefficients of these variables are zero at the same time). The issue then is: which variables are redundant, and which aren't?

Often, it's going to be a hard choice. All variables are of low quality in terms of their explanatory power, yet they contain some grains of useful information, spread over several variables and hidden in lots of noise. In order to get a good grip on the situation, it's therefore advisable to check for *multicollinearity* issues. If two or more variables are highly correlated, they produce a lot of noise, increase standard errors, and therefore make diagnostic testing for redundancy more difficult. So we should first address the multicollinearity.

If the problem remains (we have several variables that are individually insignificant, but jointly significant), we have to ask ourselves if these variables are merely control variables, or a cornerstone in solving our research question; also see the next section.

d. Remedy

If you decide that a single variable is redundant, confirmed by a t-test, remove it from the model. Done.

If you decide that several variables are redundant, and the F-test confirms that, remove them. Done.

But if you come to the conclusion that a set of variables are redundant on an individual basis, but that there is some explanatory power in the combination (a rejection of the null of redundancy by the F-test), but you cannot pinpoint it down to specific variables, you could consider PCA: Principle Component Analysis. This is a mathematical device that reduces a set of variables (say 10) to a lower number of new variables (say 3) that are uncorrelated with each other, allowing for a model with less multicollinearity. The big disadvantage is that the new variables are intricate combinations of the old, so you cannot easily say what they represent anymore. If no-one is going to care about the exact nature of control variables, for example with forecasting (see Chapter 11), this would be acceptable. Applying PCA to variables that we were interested in due to our research question is inadvisable – interpretation of the results becomes too messy.

e. Overview: omitted variable

Practical issues:

- It should be noted that any significance level is an arbitrary choice, and that all results – including p-values – are estimated. Making a decision purely on the numbers is not always a good idea; there is a bit of a grey area where we have to weigh the different consequences.
- Never omit a constant. Just don't. (see the first half of this chapter).

Assumption	All relevant variables are included in the model (and no more)
Definition	No variables are redundant.
Example violation	Any independent variable that is insignificant – such as sports injuries in explaining real estate prices.
Consequences	Higher standard errors for all variables that are correlated with the redundant variable. No effect on coefficients, R^2.
Diagnosis	Single variable: t-test ; Multiple variables: F-test, preferably re-do the test after reducing multicollinearity issues.
Remedy	Throw out any redundant variables that you can isolate (that are individually insignificant)

- While multicollinearity can be a serious issue and has to be treated as such, in many cases it will make little difference: standard errors are often either so small or so high that the conclusion will not change if a reasonable degree of multicollinearity is added. On the other hand, omitted variable bias can be quite detrimental to your results, so often the advice is, when in doubt, to err on the side of caution and leave the variable in.

Webcasts

Relevant webcasts for this chapter are:

5. The F-test

6. Transforming data

9. Faulty standard errors (heteroskedasticity & serial correlation)

Even unbiased coefficient estimates are not sufficient to conclude there is a relation between the dependent and independent variables. As we've seen before, the tool to determine whether or not such a relation exists is the t-test, which has 3 inputs:

$$t - score = \frac{Coefficient\ value - value\ under\ null\ hypothesis}{standard\ error}$$

For the test to be meaningful, all three inputs must be correct. The coefficient value has been discussed; next input, the value under the null-hypothesis is taken to be zero so we have a test that does what it's supposed to do, namely, check the existence of a relation (we try to reject the null that there is no effect of X on Y; if the t-score exceeds the critical value, say 2, the null is rejected and we therefore assume the relation exists; see chapter 4).

The third input of the t-test is the standard error of the coefficient under investigation. This standard error can be biased in its own right, even if the coefficient values are not; to see how this might happen we have to look at the assumptions of *homoskedasticity* and the *absence of serial correlation*. (See table 7.1, second assumption)

Before we turn to the definition of these terms, a quick reminder of the possible consequences. Suppose we have

Sales = 500 + 2.25 advertising budget (in thousands) + e

Now if the standard error of the slope is 1.8, it's clear that we cannot reject the standard H_0; there would be no relation between advertising budget and sales, an embarrassing situation for that department. [the calculation: $(2.25 - 0)/1.8 = 1.25$, with a p-value of 21%) However, if the standard error turns out to be only 0.75, no-one will be able to use these figures to attack the marketing strategy, as the effect is now all but certain with a t-score of 3, implying a p-value of around 1%. It's quite common that, after corrections to standard errors have been made, conclusions change too.

The source of bias in standard errors lies in the structure of the residual terms. We have two assumptions that relate to this: homoskedasticity (its opposite term, heteroskedasticity is used to denote the problem that arises from violations of the assumption) and the absence of serial correlation, which will be discussed in turn.

Homoskedasticity

a.   Definition of the problem, example

Homoskedasticity (first part of the second assumption) literally means that the variance – the spread around the mean, see chapter 4) of the residual terms is constant.

$$\sigma_\varepsilon^2 = constant$$

We can see the residuals as an indication of how closely a single observation fits the model we're estimating. On average these residuals must be zero, but individual residuals may exhibit a big spread around that mean value (which perfectly matches the definition of variance). A bigger variance of the residuals suggests the model is less reliable, as it produces bigger standard errors, see chapter 4. But it is also possible that the variance of the residuals is not constant, and therefore not every part of the dataset is equally reliable.

This becomes much clearer if we look at a residual plot which the kind of heteroskedasticity typical in financial data:

Figure 9.1

A residual plot with (mild) heteroskedasticity. We see that for example the 1983-87 and 1993-97 periods had fairly low variance - the residuals are close to the mea;, see for example how often we stay within the bandwith indicated by the dotted lines. On the other hand, we see a much more turbulent period after 1999. Depending on the type of data you're looking at (e.g. IT stocks or financials) the residuals in the 1999-2001 or the 2008+ period may be the most noteworthy. One or two big spikes does not necessarily indicate a changed variance, but if the volatility persists for quite a while- as in those two crises - it indicates heteroskedasticity.

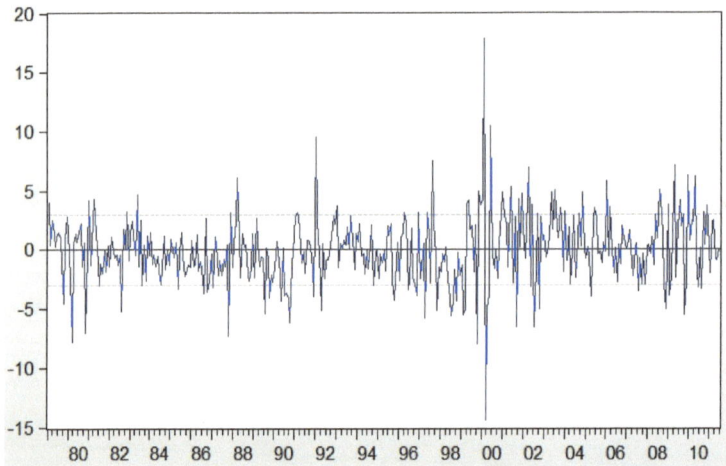

It is no coincidence that variance was very high after the bursting of the tech bubble, during the aftermath of 9/11 and the credit crisis. The reason for this is not primarily that those periods were quite turbulent for the financial markets. The issue here is the behavior of the residuals, and if our model would be capable of explaining returns just as well in turbulent times as in calmer ones, the variance of the residuals would be constant. The key is of course that these turbulent periods see markets react on all kinds of factors that are *not* normally part of your model, and hence increase your residuals. Our model gets a worse fit. And if the residuals increase, the spread around the fixed mean of zero (see the practical notes of chapter 8) has to increase as well – and we have heteroskedasticity.

The lesson we can learn from this is: as soon as the data contains many swings that aren't explained by variables in the model, they will end up in the residuals, and unless the swings are always of the same magnitude, will cause heteroskedasticity.

b. consequences

The unequal reliability of the residuals is the root of the problem, as the more unreliable parts should have a relatively bigger influence on the overall standard errors (again, just as with the R^2, it's the square of the deviations that count, and that means big errors count disproportionally heavy).

However, OLS fails to take this into account – it assumes equal reliability, that is, homoskedasticity. Consequently, your standard errors are biased. As the residuals for individual observations are fine, there's no effect on your coefficients, and therefore none on the R^2 either.

c. Diagnosis

The diagnostic test of choice for homoskedasticity is the White-test (there are many alternatives, but the concept is the same). It works by taking the squared residuals as dependent variable in an auxiliary regression (squared residuals are directly related to the variance, as the mean of the residuals is zero, see chapter 6). If the assumption is valid, the squared residuals are constant, so only the intercept of such a regression would be significant; but if the slope-coefficients of such a regression are significant, we have a violation, i.e. heteroskedasticity.

In principle, you could throw in any set of independent variables in this auxiliary regression (they should all be insignificant). Normally we'd limit ourselves to the independent variables of the original regression and their squared values (to capture non-linear relations); this is based on the presumption that if there is a pattern in the data, this pattern will most likely be found in the variables we used in our model – as they should capture all relevant influences.

So, if our original model is

$Y = a + b_1 * X_1 + b_2 * X_2 + e$

The auxiliary regression to detect heteroskedasticity becomes:

$e^2 = c + d_1 * X_1 + d_2 * X_1^2 + d_3 * X_2 + d_4 * X_2^2 + u$

The formal White test can be conducted in two ways: either we take the R^2 of this auxiliary regression (if only the intercept is relevant, the R^2 will be zero, see chapter 4), and multiply it by the number of observations, and compare the result with a Chi-square distribution. The alternative is simply an F-test on the joint significance of all independent variables.

In EVIEWS this test can be found as follows:

- In the window that contains your regression results, click on 'view'.
- Choose 'residual diagnostics', then 'Heteroskedasticity tests'.
- Out of the options, select 'White'.

The next page contains an illustration of the output.

d. Remedy

To fix the heteroskedasticity problem, we need to actively take the differing reliabilities of the residuals into account. If we replace σ_ε^2 in the formula to calculate standard errors with a weighted average of squared residuals, where the weight depends on the reliability, we would once again have unbiased standard errors. The only difficulty is in finding the proper weights.

Figure 9.2

An example of the output of the diagnostic test for heteroskedasticity.

Heteroskedasticity Test: White

F-statistic	381.9112	Prob. F(9,194)	0.0000
Obs*R-squared	193.1011	Prob. Chi-Square(9)	0.0000
Scaled explained SS	1547.605	Prob. Chi-Square(9)	0.0000

Test Equation:
Dependent Variable: RESID^2
Method: Least Squares
Date: 02/29/12   Time: 22:09
Sample: 1986M01 2002M12
Included observations: 204

Variable	Coefficient	Std. Error	t-Statistic	Prob.
C	5.401290	19.94009	0.270876	0.7868
MARKET	-2.837281	0.896926	-3.163340	0.0018
MARKET^2	0.101297	0.006802	14.89299	0.0000
MARKET*VIX	-0.048910	0.025869	-1.890655	0.0602
MARKET*WTI	0.158336	0.034296	4.616783	0.0000
VIX	0.854806	0.794845	1.075437	0.2835
VIX^2	-0.009415	0.010391	-0.906079	0.3660
VIX*WTI	0.006135	0.032696	0.187630	0.8514
WTI	-1.208926	1.376644	-0.878169	0.3809
WTI^2	0.025329	0.030887	0.820054	0.4132

R-squared	0.946574	Mean dependent var	12.84974
Adjusted R-squared	0.944096	S.D. dependent var	52.60347
S.E. of regression	12.43762	Akaike info criterion	7.927106
Sum squared resid	30010.71	Schwarz criterion	8.089759
Log likelihood	-798.5648	Hannan-Quinn criter.	7.992902
F-statistic	381.9112	Durbin-Watson stat	2.259727
Prob(F-statistic)	0.000000		

Thankfully, we do not need to find those weights ourselves; the so-called White-algorithm will do this for us, and make the necessary corrections to the standard errors in EVIEWS. (Note: this is a standard feature of EVIEWS, but strangely enough many SPSS versions do not have this tool, nor does Excel). As the inner workings of the algorithm require quite a bit of math, these are omitted here.

The sequence in EVIEWS is as follows:

- In the window where you enter your equation, go to the tab 'options'
- From the drop down list under 'coefficient covariance matrix', select 'white'
- Estimate your model.

You'll see an additional line in your output, with the notification 'White heteroskedasticity-consistent standard errors and covariance', this indicate the White-algorithm has used its own weights to account for heteroskedasticity. Apart from this, *only* the standard errors have changed. This is as it should be; heteroskedasticity does not affect the coefficients (and therefore the residuals remain the same, as does the R^2).

e. Overview: heteroskedasticity

Assumption	Homoskedasticity
Definition	Variance of the residuals is constant
Example violation	Virtually all financial data, a poorer fit in turbulent times creates higher variances
Consequences	Bias in standard errors, everything else unaffected
Diagnosis	White test
Remedy	White- or Newey-West algorithms in Eviews.

Practical issues:

- Testing for heteroskedasticity: the $n*R^2$ test and the F-test usually give almost identical solutions, except in small samples. If either indicates heteroskedasticity, we might as well correct for it.
- Later Eviews versions tend to incorporate yet a third measure, the "Scaled explained SS", which can be ignored if it contradicts the other two (as it sometimes will).
- One can also include *cross-terms* in the auxiliary regression; these would add another term to the auxiliary regression: $d_5*X_1*X_2$. Such additional terms - if we have 3 or more variables in our original model, the number of cross-terms increases - may help to detect more heteroskedasticity, but may cause problems in small dataset as the auxiliary regression can only be used as long as we have more observations than coefficients we have to estimate; cross-terms can cause this number to increase rapidly.
- Correcting heteroskedasticity: if the White or Newey-west algorithms are applied in datasets with heteroskedasticity, the effect is usually negligible. It looks poor to apply the correction without testing, but in this particular case it still beats the alternative of never testing and therefore continue with biased standard errors.

Serial correlation

a. Definition of the problem, example

The absence of serial correlation (part of assumption 2) can be defined as follows: there is no relation between a residual (error term) in one period and residuals from a previous period.

$$Correlation\left(e_t, e_{t-k,}\right) = 0$$

Note that k can be 1 (denoting the residual one period back), but also larger, in which case we go further back in time.

In fact, this assumption means that errors in our model are one-off affairs; the model might predict wrongly in one period, but this error will have no influence on the error in the subsequent (or previous) period.

The most common way to violate this assumption is to include (unmodeled) seasonal effects in your data. If, for example, your business is much stronger during boom markets (e.g. mergers and acquisitions), a model that does not include the state of the economy will overestimate during recessions, and underestimate when the economy is strong. As these situations tend to last for several periods, the same mistake is repeated several times in a row, which means that residuals will be related and you'll have serial correlation.

Again, this becomes much clearer if we look at a residual plot (in a stylized example, the seasonal effects are bigger than the random variation here, which is not necessarily the case):

Figure 9.3
A residual plot with (very severe) serial correlation. We see a very pronounced seasonal movement, indicating that the unmodeled seasonal aspects are in fact stronger than the other sources of the residual.

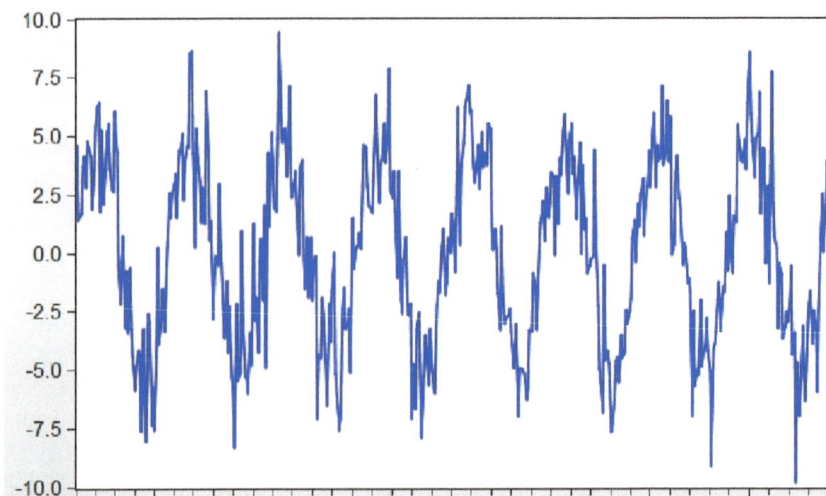

We see a recurring pattern in these residuals, based on a couple of previous values for the error term you can make a fairly accurate prediction of the error term in a future period. Note that this graph shows an effect that's more pronounced than most cases of serial correlation. The degree of serial correlation depends on the correlation coefficient between the current residual and its predecessor. At a value of zero, the problem is absent, at values close to 1 or -1 it becomes very severe. Note that values beyond that range are by definition impossible:

$$-1 \leq Correlation\left(e_t, e_{t-1,}\right) \leq 1$$

b. Consequences

As with heteroskedasticity, the unequal reliability of the residuals is the root of the problem. In particular cases where shocks (unexpected big residuals) occur that are also contained in subsequent residuals pose problems. The proper weights became harder to establish, as part of the residual is due to earlier shocks, which therefore should have different weights.

An illustration of this effect can be seen in Figure 9.3 below, which shows the effects of a single shock with various degrees of serial correlation. Note that if the correlation is negative, the residuals will oscillate.

The consequences for *serial correlation* are limited to biased standard errors, with the same problem of unequal reliability at work (in case you decide to do some further reading: this topic is usually addressed as an issue with the '(variance-)covariance matrix' in more advanced texts). The residuals for individual observations are affected by shocks, yet in bigger samples these effects will average out and your coefficients will remain unbiased, with no effect on the R^2 either. In very small samples, however, this argument may not hold.

Figure 9.4

A stylized set of residuals after one shock, whose effects remain relevant for several periods after the shock. the extent depends on the correlation coefficient (often denoted by the symbol ρ).

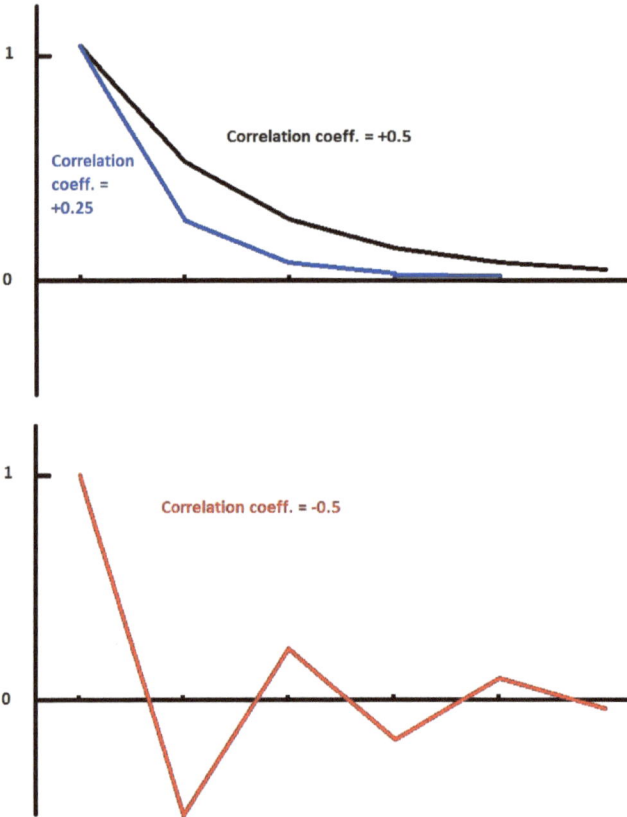

c. Diagnosis

The diagnostic test of choice for serial correlation is the Breusch-Godfrey LM -test. As before, it tries to establish a pattern in the residuals – if the pattern exists, we have a violation of the corresponding assumption and we'll need to take action. The residuals (unmodified) are taken as dependent variable in the auxiliary regression, lagged values – that is, residuals from previous periods – are taken as the independent variables:

$e = c + d_1 * X_1 + ... + d_2 * e_{t-1} + d_3 * e_{t-2} + ... + u$

If the OLS-assumptions are valid, none of the parameters in this auxiliary regression are significant; but the opposite holds too: if the slope-coefficients of such a regression are in fact significant, this indicates a problem. If the slope coefficients for previous values of the residual (d_2, d_3 in the example above) are significant, the correlation between them deviates from zero and therefore our regression will suffer from serial correlation.

So our diagnostic test is a test for the joint significance of all slope-parameters (a significant intercept is a violation of a different assumption, that the average error is zero). Again, there are two ways of performing usch a test: either we take the R^2 of this auxiliary regression (if only the intercept is relevant, the R^2 will be zero, see chapter 4), and multiply it by the number of observations, and compare the result with a Chi-square distribution. The alternative is simply an F-test on the joint significance of all independent variables (you may note that the original independent variables such as X1 are present in the auxiliary regression too, but those coefficients should also be zero based on the absence of endogeneity – see the next chapter).

An example of the EVIEWS-output is on the next page.

To get this output, us the sequence in EVIEWS:

- In the window that contains your regression results, click on 'view'.
- Choose 'residual diagnostics', then 'Serial Correlation LM test'.
- Then specifiy how many lags you want to include (default 2, as was used in the figure below, this matter is discussed after the figure).

Breusch-Godfrey Serial Correlation LM Test:

F-statistic	667.1405	Prob. F(2,584)	0.0000
Obs*R-squared	410.3808	Prob. Chi-Square(2)	0.0000

Test Equation:
Dependent Variable: RESID
Method: Least Squares
Sample: 1 590
Included observations: 590
Presample missing value lagged residuals set to zero.

Variable	Coefficient	Std. Error	t-Statistic	Prob.
X1	-1.561855	0.854089	-1.828678	0.0680
X2	-1.274474	3.937155	-0.323704	0.7463
X3	1.059182	0.538047	1.968567	0.0495
C	3.834126	2.094737	1.830362	0.0677
RESID(-1)	0.637874	0.040153	15.88614	0.0000
RESID(-2)	0.228487	0.040116	5.695678	0.0000

R-squared	0.695561	Mean dependent var	2.42E-15
Adjusted R-squared	0.692954	S.D. dependent var	9.692774
S.E. of regression	5.370932	Akaike info criterion	6.209997
Sum squared resid	16846.59	Schwarz criterion	6.254541
Log likelihood	-1825.949	Hannan-Quinn criter.	6.227350
F-statistic	266.8562	Durbin-Watson stat	1.934924
Prob(F-statistic)	0.000000		

A recurring issue is how many lags to include in our test. After all, if we have a sufficiently large dataset, we could use not just the residuals from the previous period, but add the residuals of two periods back as well, and so on till we run out of data. This is not desirable; if we throw in enough lags – additional variables in our auxiliary regression – it will become harder and harder to reject the null hypothesis, even if it is in fact false. The reason for this is the chance-element in hypothesis testing: if you test 50 hypotheses which are all wrong, there is still a good chance of not rejecting one or several – we always accept a certain probability (usually 5%, see chapter 4) that our conclusion is wrong, since certainty is not on offer.

On the other hand, if the serial correlation is of a high order – if you have a yearly pattern in monthly data for example, the correlation between a residual and the residual 12 months back will be high – you might not even be able to detect the problem if you include a low number of lags. It's clear we have to find a balance: include enough to find the problem, but not so many as to drown out faint evidence under a pile of noise.

Practical advice in this matter would be:
- to include at least as many lags to move to the next logical frequency. If your data is daily, check for 7 lags to identify effects that surface once a week. Use 5 days if you're looking at business / trading days only. If it's monthly, go for 12. If it's quarterly, check for at least 4 lags, and so on.
- check not just the outcome of the test as a whole, but also the p-values of the individual slope-coefficients. If there are one or more which are not significant but still quite low (say 15%) it might pay off to test for fewer lags as well. In case your first test had a dozen lags or more, also rerun the test with fewer lags to be sure. It takes just a few seconds.

d. Remedy

In fixing serial correlation, our prime concern is adjusting the standard errors so that they become unbiased. Again, we need to sort out the proper weights of each residual, taking the differing reliabilities into account. (This is merely addressing the symptoms rather than the problem; it is possible to model the structure of the residuals explicitly and thereby purging the model of its effects, however for all practical purposes the result is the same). The link with heteroskedasticity can be exploited here; a different, more flexible weighting algorithm – the Newey-West algorithm – is able to rid our standard errors of biases due to both serial correlation and heteroskedasticity.

The sequence in Eviews is therefore:

- In the window where you enter your equation, go to the tab 'options'
- From the drop down list under 'coefficient covariance matrix', select 'HAC (Newey-West)'
- Estimate your model.

You'll see an additional line in your output, with the notification 'HAC standard errors and covariance', this indicate the Newey-West-algorithm has been used to calculate standard errors. Again, no other changes are made – nor need to be, the coefficients are unaffected (and therefore the residuals remain usable, as does the R^2).

e. Overview: serial correlation

Practical issues:

- Serial correlation testing may appear counter-intuitive for cross-sections (data without a time-component, such as a dataset with one observation per company and several variables with info on those companies), but it depends on the nature of the dataset if it is relevant. For example, if your data does not contain observations over time but over different sectors of industry or markets, the logical order that is needed for testing would not come in the form of a time-dimension. Yet it may be present in – for example – a geographical dimension: increased competition in one region may influence the sales in adjoining regions. This mechanism could also create a relation between residuals, and would require the same correction. Always bear in mind that the procedure to calculate your standard errors doesn't know nor care about any logical ordering; in fact, we could even turn it around by saying that as soon as you do find serial correlation (which is not due to chance, which is also always a possibility) there must be some sort of mechanism at work that connects the observations.

Assumption	Absence of serial correlation
Definition	Residuals are uncorrelated with residuals from previous periods
Example violation	Seasonal effects (in the independent variable but not in the dependent one, or vice versa)
Consequences	Bias in standard errors, everything else unaffected (if sample is moderately large, say $n>30$)
Diagnosis	Breusch-Godfrey LM test
Remedy	Newey-West algorithm in Eviews.

- As with heteroskedasticity, the Breuch-Godfrey test is based on an $n*R^2$ test and an F-test, which usually give very identical solutions, except in small samples. If either indicates serial correlation, a correction is called for.
- Standard EVIEWS output also contains another measure for serial correlation, the Durbin-Watson (DW) test. This test only considers first order serial correlation. It doesn't come with a p-value, but any value below 1.5 or above 2.5 is regarded as significant serial correlation. DW test statistics very close to 0 or 4 (the test produces values in the 0-4 range, with 2 indicating no first order serial correlation) are usually a result of a specification problem, for example a dependent variable measured as a price level, while the independent variable is a return.
- Correcting for serial correlation: this is always done by means of the Newey-West algorithm. This also corrects for heteroskedasticity; yet since the correction is harmless if the underlying problem doesn't

exist, one can apply the Newey-West algorithm also when there is only serial correlation and no heteroskedasticity.

Webcasts

Through www.covariance.nl you can find a series of webcasts that will help you with EVIEWS. Relevant webcasts for this chapter are:

7. Heteroskedasticity

8. Serial correlation

Conclusion

Both heteroskedasticity and serial correlation are problems related to the residuals of your models; these residuals have a non-standard structure which means the standard errors can be biased – and therefore the reliability of your results may be impaired. Both problems are diagnosed using an auxiliary regression which test for patterns in the residuals; the residuals themselves become the dependent variable in case of serial correlation, while the White-test uses the squared residuals (and in fact their variance). If the null of a pattern in the (squared) residuals is not rejected, the OLS assumptions are met and we can safely use our standard errors.

From this we can see that neither problem will emerge if the residuals are well behaved, so sudden changes in variance or seasonal patterns, which are present in both the dependent and an independent variable of your original model, do not cause problems. Only when the pattern is present on the left-hand side of the equation but not on the right hand (except for the residuals), or vice versa, will we see a violation of these assumptions.

A fix for both problems is straightforward: we have to weigh the residuals in a different manner, to compensate for the differences in reliability. This can be done using the White-algorithm (heteroskedasticity only) or the Newey-West-algorithm (both heteroskedasticity and serial correlation). Only the standard errors will change as a consequence, the coefficients remain the same, as they were unbiased to begin with. Once the model has been re-estimated with these options, both coefficients and standard errors are safe to use again, and we can draw our conclusions based on t-tests in the customary manner.

10. Biased coefficients revisited: errors-in-variables and endogeneity

We've seen that excluding a relevant variable from the model leads to biased coefficients: the relations between independent and dependent variables are not really what they seem, because our parameters are wrong (chapter 8). However, omitted variables are not the only way to get into trouble with biased coefficients.

The two other problems are errors-in-variables, and endogeneity. The first is what the name says: your input data is faulty, and this will have its effects on the output. The second problem is one of causality: we normally assume cause and effect are embedded in distinct variables. But real data does not always fit this pattern: feedback effects may cause X to influence Y, but also Y to influence X.

While the latter problem could be seen as a special case of the first (we lack a 'clean' independent variable in both cases, instead we only have an approximation of the variable we'd really want to use), this overlap is only visible in more abstract representations; we'll consequently deal with both assumptions separately.

Errors-in-variables

a.   Definition of the problem, example

The most down to earth definition is simply that a variable is not measuring what it is supposed to measure. The difference is an error; this error could be random (sometimes your data consists of values that are too low, and others that are too high, without any pattern), systematic (every time you get a number, it's off by a fixed percentage or amount), or both.

Interestingly enough, the systematic errors are often ignored. The reason is that they will have no influence on your predictions as long as the data you use to construct these predictions has the same systematic error. For example, suppose the exchange rate between euros and dollars were fixed at 1.5 to 1. It would not matter one bit for the quality of your regression if you translated all amounts into the other currency, as long as you keep doing it for all data, past, present and future. Even more prosaic: if you want a model that explains your profit in dollars, but all data is measured in cents, your systematic error is a factor 100, but the effect on your predicted profit is zero.

So the more precise definition of the problem is that we have a *random* error in our variables.

This could be due to any number of causes, from typos (human error) to poor accounting (poor procedures to check data) to people giving desirable rather than truthful answers (deception). The case where our variable is in fact an approximation of what we want to measure – but the data we really want is unobservable – also falls in this category.

b. Consequences

The consequences differ if the errors are present in the dependent variable or the independent one. In fact, if the errors are in the dependent (y) variable, it will simply lead to higher residuals (and therefore higher standard errors), but as long as the error is on average zero, the coefficients are unbiased (if the error is not zero on average, you will see an effect in the estimated intercept).

The situation is more severe if the errors are (also) present in your independent (x-) variable. This will not only lead to biased intercept and slope coefficients, but we can see (from the formula) that the bias is not influenced by the sample size.

$$Bias = -\frac{\text{slope coeff.} * \text{Variance} (u_j)}{\text{Variance} (\hat{x}_j)}$$

Where the variance of u indicates the variance of your measurement errors, and the variance of $\hat{x}_j$ is the variance of your independent variable (including errors). So the bigger your errors relative to the variable that contains them, the bigger your bias.

This formula also shows that the number of observations drops out of the equation. So no matter how much data we have, the bias remains – our estimated coefficients are *inconsistent* as well. It should be noted that together with a bias for every size of the dataset, this also affects the standard errors (as they are calculated using residuals which are in turn calculated using biased coefficients, so the end result is distorted).

c. Diagnosis

Errors-in-variables are notoriously hard to test for. Any statistical test compares the data to a certain benchmark (the null hypothesis) and then judges if the difference is large enough to rule out that the discrepancy is caused by random movements. With errors-in-variables, we do not have such a benchmark. The only proper comparison would be with the correct data. However, if we know the correct values, we wouldn't be using the ones with (possible) errors to begin with! Practically speaking, we therefore never have the data to conduct a proper diagnostic test.

However, should we somehow have data on the same variable that we believe is error-free, we could simply test (by means of an F-test) if the coefficients of the model with the second set of data are the same as with the original (but perhaps erroneous) data. In reality, finding such a difference simply results in a discussion about which dataset is more likely to be correct, especially since every collection of empirical data points might have some sort of random error in it, especially if the data comes from human respondents or collectors.

It should be noted that this issue has not prevented virtually all of the sciences and many practitioners from using regression analysis. We simply have to make do with what we can get, en attempt to ensure our data is as error-free as possible.

d. Remedy

The same fundamental problem we faced when finding a diagnostic test plagues us in finding a remedy: in general, there is no certainty that a dataset is error-free, and there's rarely any external evidence that one possible set of data is better than another alternative. Fixing this problem is therefore mainly a matter of prevention.

A few general rules can be given in this respect:

Make sure the data is checked and double checked if compiled from another source. Coding errors and typo's are rife in most big datasets. It's usually worthwhile to pay for properly checked and compiled datasets (in some sectors, Finance for instance, vast commercial databases are available; some parties, such as Bloomberg, have made providing quality data their business model, and thrive because of it).

Try to eliminate the human factor, if possible. If the data is directly available from some sort of computerized system, try to work with those numbers directly rather than have an additional (human and therefore fallible) element in the interface. A structural flaw – the kind of errors computers make - is usually easier to fix, and has less severe consequences, than random deviations.

Try to confirm your data from various sources. It's unlikely that two independent datasets will agree completely, but if they are nearly identical, it offers some peace of mind, as the chance of big random errors is lower.

e. Overview: errors-in-variables

Assumption	There are no errors-in-variables.
Definition	Input data is free of random errors.
Example violation	Any type of random mishaps in collecting or processing data, from 'don't know' answers from respondents to typos.
Consequences	Bias in coefficients, estimation procedure is inconsistent. Standard errors biased as a result of the bias in coefficients
Diagnosis	None, unless you have an alternative dataset you know is error-free. In that case, just use that one.
Remedy	See diagnosis. Take preventative measures to control the problem as much as possible.

Practical issues:
- The error-in-variables argument can be used to question almost all empirical research, up to a point. As a consequence, it lacks the power to convince unless it can be shown to be a particularly severe case. Moreover, the analyst usually can do very little to remove the problem.
- In case you are quite worried about this problem, it might be worthwhile to do some sensitivity analysis: consider what magnitude of errors are likely given how your data was collected, and add a comparable amount of random noise to your data (the essential part is that the variance of the error is well chosen), and look at the effects. It must be noted however that can be hard to get a realistic estimate of the variance you need for this method; experience pays off in this respect.

Endogeneity

a. Definition of the problem, examples

On a practical level, *endogeneity* is nothing else than the question which came first, the chicken or the egg. In our framework this means that not only X is influencing Y (the independent variable causes[3] changes in the dependent variable) but the reverse also happens: changes in the dependent variable influence X. As X is supposed to be independent, this is a violation of the basic assumptions.

On a theoretical level, the problem can be defined as a correlation between the residuals of the regression and the independent variable. This correlation should be zero, according to the Gauss-Markov Theorem:

Corralation (X,e) = 0

The best way to look at this issue is to regard it as a case of simultaneous equations; we're going to model how X influences Y (our normal model) but add a second equation where X is a function of Y:

$Y = a + b_1 * X + e$

$X = c + d_1 * Y + u$

Different letters from the usual a, b and e are used in the second equation to emphasize the difference with the first.

Let's use two examples to illustrate this.

In Finance, one requires a higher rate of return for a more risky investment. So a company that is more at risk in adverse markets will need to pay a higher interest on its loans, and its stock should have a higher expected return. Generally, this risk is measured by finding the influence of the market (a broad stock index) on the value of the stock.

---

[3] In this chapter, I use any term derived from 'causality' as any non-specialist would, without implying a more technical definition.

return stock = a + b*return market +e

Yet in case of big businesses, it's quite possible that news regarding the company moves the markets. If a big retailer announces a very good or very bad quarter, this would be seen as an important signal about the state of the economy, and influence all stock prices, and therefore the market.

Return market = c + d*return stock +u

From macro-economics, we know that savings depend on how much money is earned – at higher levels of income, one could save more. This income depends in part on productivity; a higher level of efficiency in production allows for higher incomes. But in the aggregate (over an entire market), productivity depends also on how much savings are available as this determines the price of loans needed to invest in the equipment needed to obtain a higher productivity. So we have 3 relations:

Savings = a+b*income+u

Income = c +d*productivity +v

Productivity =e+f*savings+w

It is clear that a shock in any of the variables will have effects on all others, as each variable is to be found both on the right-hand side of the equation (as a supposedly independent variable), but also on the left-hand side (dependent variable).

This situation, called a system of *simultaneous equations* (because one has to consider the interactions and therefore all equations must be estimated simultaneously) is the most common way for endogeneity to present itself. It is not limited to macro-economic models, likewise, any situation where buyers and sellers have to decide how much of a service or product to trade at which price also leads to a simultaneous equation problem:

Suppose that due to quality demands, only one supplier is available for a certain product, while there are many small buyers. The buyers adjust the quantity they buy according to the price of the product; if the product is expensive, they buy less, if the product is cheap, they buy more. Now the seller of this same product will observe a certain demand and set its price accordingly, assuming he needs a certain overall margin to cover all costs (fixed and variable). In all, the seller can set the price, which has implications for the quantity, the buyers have no noticeable impact on price but can vary their quantity. In formulas:

Buyers: quantity = a+b*price+e

Seller: price = c+d*quantity+u

Again we have a simultaneous equations problem. Of course, in a more realistic setup there would be alternative suppliers, buyers may have an impact on the price as well, and so on, but this only adds complexity, and will not negate the problem outlined above.

b. Consequences

On an intuitive level, it's obvious that endogeneity will have consequences for your coefficients and their reliability. Our independent (X) variable is 'contaminated' by influence from Y; as an example we could say we might have two equations: Y=3X but also X=2Y to account for the feedback effect. Now if we would isolate Y in this second model, the result would be Y=0.5X, which is a completely different value! This does not bode well for the reliability of your coefficients, but in fact the problem runs deeper: as only one direction of the effect (from X to Y) is included in the regression model, all feedback effects are ignored which causes bias in the coefficients themselves; the numbers we get are (on average) wrong.

The result is a bias, which depends on the covariance between x and the residuals (the covariance is based on the correlation between X and e) and the variance of X:

$$Bias = -\frac{\text{Covariance } (x, e)}{\text{Variance } (x)}$$

So whatever happens, this bias will only disappear if the correlation between X and e vanishes, so if we solve the chicken-and-egg problem.

Again, it should be noted that a bias in the coefficients will also affect the residuals, and thereby the standard errors and the R^2.

c. Diagnosis

The core of the problem is a relationship between residuals and independent variables. Normally, we would try to map this correlation – it's easily calculated – and test if it is so different from zero that we'd have to reject that null hypothesis, and that would be our diagnostic test. Yet this approach will *not* work, as the bias in our coefficients will also translate into different residuals; their correlation is in a sense also biased. This makes a direct test on the correlation impossible.

Endogeneity can only be tested through the use of additional variables that are highly correlated with the original data, and poorly correlated with the residuals – those variables would capture the change due to endogeneity. As we need such variables also to fix the problem, the diagnostic test is discussed after the remedy-section.

d. Remedy

The essential element of fixing endogeneity is finding variables that work in only one direction; the simultaneous equations problem should be replaced by one where all independent variables are indeed independent (of the y-variables). The alternative - estimating the entire system in one go - is sometimes feasible, but beyond the scope of this book.

This means we have to look out for new data to replace our endogeneity-stricken variables. The most straightforward approach is replacement of the old variables with new ones, called instrumental variables. These *instrumental variables* (IVs) need to be highly correlated with the original data it will replace – so as little as possible of the information we need is lost – but it must not be correlated with the residuals of the original endogenous regression, or we would have the same problem all over again.

Figure 10.1

Characteristics of a good IV.

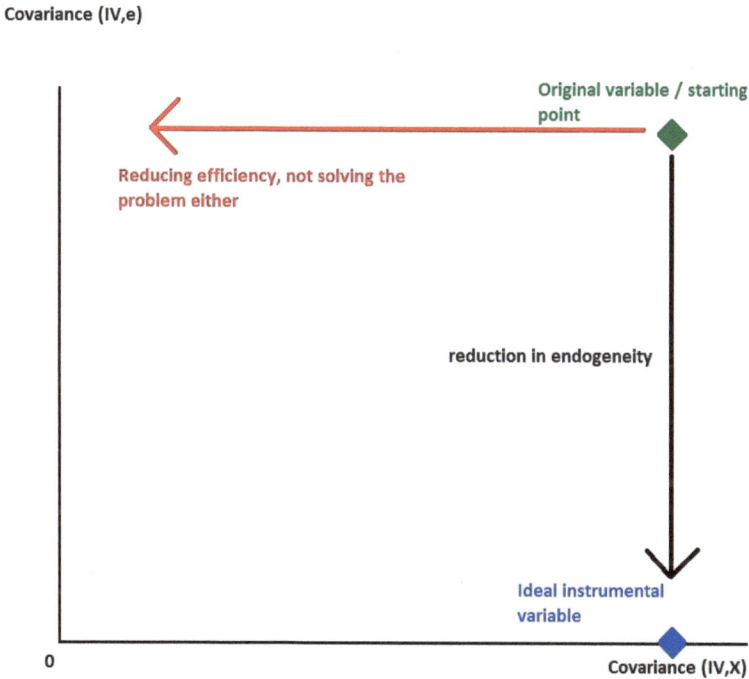

It should be noted that we tend to replace independent variables, not the dependent ones, as the general question of regression analysis is always: what does explain Y? If we start replacing Y with another variable, we're not answering the same question anymore, and it is doubtful our output will be useful at all. So we want to tackle the problem by finding an IV for our independent variables that are affected by endogeneity.

Concerns about finding an IV-candidate are discussed at the end of the section under 'Practical Issues'.

Next, once we have found a candidate for an IV, we often want to make it as similar to the old data as possible. After all, if we are looking to explain income (see the second example above), but have to replace productivity as an endogenous variable – for example by the amount of hours worked, which would have little relation to savings – we still want to know the magnitude and significance of the coefficient for productivity. Without any rescaling, we'll get a number that is meaningless in that context. We need to translate our raw IV data to estimated values of the original variable. This means that our IV is going to change; we're adjusted numbers. Interestingly, this rescaling can be done by an auxiliary regression:

Suppose we start with this (endogenous) equation:

Original = a +bIV_raw+e   (Income = c +d*productivity +v)

Then your proper IV is g+h*IV_raw, (hours worked_rescaled = g+h*productivity) and these numbers are the ones to be inserted into your new regression:

Y = a + b*IV_proper + e (income = a+b* hours worked_rescaled)

However, it is quite possible that finding a good IV is impossible, either due to lack of data or because the interaction is too complex (when you need several variables in combination to produce an IV).

In such cases, the method explained above can be expanded to Two-Stage Least Square (2SLS) estimation. This allows you to use any set of variables, including your original data. In fact, often you will see better performance from a combination of variables in constructing the IV, so 2SLS is in many cases preferable over replacing a variable with an IV.

The method involves again two regressions, first to estimate the instrument, then estimating the final regression with the relations we're interested in.

An example (where all coefficients have different letters or subscripts, as they are never the same numbers):

Advertisement = $a+b_1$*sales+ b_2*competition+ b_3*cost of commercials+e

Sales = $c+d_1$*advertisement+ d_2*competition+ d_3*interest rate+ d_4*hourly wages

These equations state that advertisements efforts are determed by sales and the activity of the competition. However, sales depend on advertisements, competition as well as interest rates (suppose we have a product usually bought on credit) and hourly wages. NB: in reality the situation would likely be more complex, involving for example different sources for the advertisement budget. The aim here is to illustrate the endogeneity.

The first stage would then be to create two IVs according to the original relations:

Estimated advertisement = f $+g_1$*advertisement+ g_2*competition+ g_3*interest rate+ g_4*hourly wages+ g_5*cost of commercials+e

Estimated Sales =k $+l_1$*advertisement+ l_2*competition+ l_3*interest rate+ l_4*hourly wages+ l_5*cost of commercials+e

Because all variables are potentially linked, all variables should be in the stage 1 equations.[4]

Then the second stage becomes:

Advertisement = a+b*Estimated_sales+c*competition+d*cost of commercials+e

---

[4] Strictly speaking, one should construct the *Reduced Form Equations* to find out which variables should be included. However, this is both tedious and complex algebra, and the inclusion of an irrelevant variable would not introduce bias in our coefficients anyway. Throwing in all variables is by far the easiest solution here.

Sales = f+g*Estimated_advertisement+h*competition+k*interest rate+l*hourly wages

This final regression is free from endogeneity. The one problem is that if the quality of the first regression is low, you can get an error-in-variables problem – your instrumental variables are also independent variables, and we have to assume they're accurate. If the R^2 of the first stage is fairly high, this is seen as an indication that this problem is limited.

c (2). Diagnosis, again.

The standard diagnostic test for endogeneity is called the Hausman test, and works by detecting the bias caused by the correlation between residual and independent variable - as the correlation itself cannot be accurately measured. This indirect test assumes that the model is correctly specified; if that is the case we can use the original equation (suspected of endogeneity) and compare this with the situation where the IVs are *added* to this original equation.

Since we assume that the model is not subject to omitted variable bias, those IVs should be completely superfluous; everything they can add in terms of explanatory power would be contained n the original variables, if they have the correct, unbiased values. If the IVs are explaining our independent variable, it must be because endogeneity is biasing the coefficients.

The Hausman test is therefore nothing else than an F-test (see chapter 4) with the null hypothesis that all the IVs have coefficients equal to zero. If this null is rejected, there is biased, which is assumed to be caused by endogeneity.

To continue our previous example:

Advertisement = $a + b_1$*sales+ b_2*competition+ b_3*cost of commercials+ b_4* Estimated Sales+e

Sales = $c + d_1$*advertisement+ d_2*competition+ d_3*interest rate+ d_4*hourly wages+ d_5* Estimated advertisement+e

The null-hypothesis would be: b4=0 and d5 is zero (which requires two separate t-tests or F-tests, as we have one IV each, a t-test is also possible)

And if the p-value is below 5%, we reject this null and conclude that we do have an endogeneity problem.

e. Overview: endogeneity

Assumption	All independent variables are exogenous
Definition	The independent variables are not influenced by the dependent ones; (the independent variables are uncorrelated with the residuals)
Example violation	A rural region sees a population decrease because of fewer facilities, or do the facilities disappear due to lack of customers?
Consequences	Bias in coefficients, estimation procedure is inconsistent. Standard errors biased as a result of the bias in coefficients
Diagnosis	Hausmann-test (an F-test using instrumental variables; if they are jointly significant there is endogeneity or misspecification)
Remedy	The use of instrumental variables, preferably in a Two-stage least Squares regression (2SLS)

Practical issues:

- Finding a good IV can be difficult. The 2SLS method offers an easy way out, but will only work if both equations are correctly specified - omitted variable bias will have a greater effect as it will distort both stages. Sometimes it may therefore be better to use the replacement method, and throw out your endogenous variable, and go for a new one instead.
- These IVs tend to be successful if the impact of the feedback effect is reduced, while maintaining the overall pattern (remember, it's the variation in the data that needs to stay the same, the average value can be rescaled and is therefore irrelevant). Good candidates are often found in industry-wide data (so total amount spend by you and all your competitors, rather than your own budget) or portfolios. In the example where a single stock may influence the market, it can pay off to use an equally weighted market index - which counts each stock equally, rather than weighs it by its share of the market value, as would be in line with financial theory. Because the weight of the stock under investigation is reduced, the feedback effect is smaller, and the endogeneity problem reduced.
- A poor IV would in fact create an errors-in-variables problem. Therefore, when applying 2SLS, the R^2 of the first stage is important: it gives you an indication of how big these errors will be.

Webcasts

Through www.covariance.nl you can find a series of webcasts that will help you with EVIEWS. Relevant webcasts for this chapter are:

5. The F-test

10. Two-stage least squares (2SLS)

Part V: What regression analysis can and cannot do for you

What remains is to review what regression analysis can and cannot do for you. The main purpose of many analyses is not just to explain the past, but to forecast the future. This is indeed possible using the techniques shown in the previous chapters, but some common sense warnings, especially regarding causality, must be heeded. If that is done, you will not only be able to perform the analysis, but also to critically judge them.

11. Forecasting

Forecasting is the art of predicting the future based on data. More to the point, we try to figure out what the value of a variable will be in the coming period. Let's call this Y_{t+1}. To create such a forecast, we can use two approaches:

A. We can try to predict other variables that influence Y, and apply the relation we already found to the future period. In terms of equations, it means we have found the coefficients of Y = a +bX+e, and with X_{t+1} we then create our forecast for Y_{t+1} as a+bX_{t+1}.

This sounds simple enough, but the main problem is of course that X_{t+1} might be just as hard to come by as Y_{t+1}. Yet in some cases this can be a fruitful approach, say for example that demand for a product depends of the percentage growth of the economy; then we only need to use one of the many forecasts that are regularly made regarding economic growth (for example by the OECD, but also various governmental organizations on a national level and private parties will publish their outlooks.)

To implement this way of forecasting, gather data on all independent variables for a representative period (note that the shorter the period, the less reliable your coefficients, but if data is used that does not reflect current conditions anymore, the coefficients will be biased). Then estimate a regression as usual:

$$y_t = a + b_1 X_{1,t} + b_2 X_{2,t} + \cdots + e$$

(as always, the index t must run from the beginning of the dataset to the final observation. So X_t denotes all observations for variable X up to the current moment (t), but X_{t+1} denotes just one number, namely the forecast for the next period. The three dots indicate that more independent variables may be added as needed)

And then, with a, b_1, b_2 etc. known, calculate Y_{t+1} as

$$y_{t+1} = a + b_1 X_{1,t+1} + b_2 X_{2,t+1}$$

In essence, all problems - and all solutions - regarding a normal regression analysis apply; if the coefficients are off, the forecast will be inaccurate as well. This is especially the case if X_{t+1} differs a lot from the average value of X_t. In such a case, errors in slope coefficients are multiplied by a very large (or very small) number, making it more likely that the final result is too large or too small. Additionally, if X_{t+1} turns out to be wrong, then this will also cause forecasting errors (this is called a conditioning error).

B. We can try to find a trend in the variable itself. This means predicting Y_{t+1} based solely on previous values of Y: y_t, Y_{t-1}, Y_{t-2} etc. The main objection here is that this method assumes there is a relation to be found in the first place. If there is a seasonal pattern, this can be a very fruitful method. If movements are random - which can be argued for liquid markets like stock exchanges or foreign currencies - previous values of Y will contain no relevant information, and the R^2 of these types of regressions will be close to zero.

Taking this route, we estimate the regression:

$$y_t = a + b_1 Y_{t-1} + b_2 Y_{t-2} + \cdots + e$$

and with a, b_1, b_2 etc. known, calculate Y_{t+1} as

$$y_{t+1} = a + b_1 Y_t + b_2 Y_{t-1}$$

With this procedure, it can be shown that there will be a bias in the slope coefficients, due to autoregression: the independent variable isn't truely independent. Thankfully, this bias decreases with the number of observations, so consistency is not lost. There is not much that can be done about this problem, unless the bias is measured (it depends on how many slope coefficients we have and their value). But in general, the argument of consistency is powerful enough, at any rate the real aim here is to reduce forecasting errors, and despite *autoregression*, a model like this will reduce forecast errors as much as possible if properly specified.

The real question is then: what will be better: we obtain a forecast of X_{t+1} externally and run it through a regression model, or try to find a trend in the y series we already have?

As always, the issue will depend on the data. A seasonal pattern or a trend (see the next chapter) will argue for a model with previous values of Y as 'independent' variables. There is also no reason why the two approaches cannot be combined. But the best argument for a forecasting procedure is that it performs well if we allow it to actually forecast things!

Hold-out sample

So it's is highly recommended to make a forecast on part of your data (say, the first K observations, with K<T, and T the total number of observations; a sensible number for K would be anywhere between 70 and 90% of your observations), and then see if that model has accurately predicted the remaining part (observations K+1 to T). The part you don't use for your forecast is the hold-out sample.

Now no model will forecast perfectly; there will be forecasting errors, that is the difference between the predicted Y and the actual Y. Some forecast errors will be small, some big, some positive, some negative. To measure the forecasting power of our regression we need to combine them. Like we did with regression residuals, we could square them, and then add them. (though it's customary to divide by the number of prediction, and then take the square root again; this is called the Root Mean Square Error, or RMSE). But it's also possible just to take the absolute value (so -7 becomes +7) and take the average of those numbers. This is called Mean absolute Deviation (MAD).

The best model is the one that produces the lowest RMSE or MAD.

A final word of caution: neither the RMSE or MAD says much about the quality of your forecast by itself. It is perfectly possible that some relations are easier to forecast than others. If a law of physics is involved, your forecast should be accurate up to the measurement error of the instruments, often a millionth or smaller of the actual effect. In business, the levels of noise will be much greater. Not all actions from competitors, fashions, scandals, innovations and so on will be in your model. Like the R^2, the absolute level depends simply on the possibilities to filter out noise, and in empirical managerial data, those are limited. What we can - and should! - do is compare different models, each producing their own forecast, and look at their relative RMSE or MAD. The playing field is not determined by any cut-off value (100 or 0.001), but by what the other models manage to produce.

12. Causality

So, you have found a relation. You R^2 is sufficient for the topic at hand, your slope coefficients are significant even after correcting for those pesky methodological problems. You might be excused for thinking you have found the variable(s) that *cause* Y. Riddle solved.

Unfortunately, life isn't so simple. The problem revolves around the word 'cause', which suggests we identified cause and effect, the 'mover' and 'moved object'. Here data analysis can look a lot better than it really is: a regression can provide you with very nice and significant results even if there is no causality involved. In fact, proving causality is very hard in real-life situations.

Here's what can happen:

There really is a causal relationship

if the relationship exists, and it is strong enough, you will find it in the data. But this is not enough; a regression compares the same period/entities over different variables. In order to distinguish a causal relation from the other possibilities - where causality is an illusion - we need some indication that X is indeed a cause, and the change in Y an effect.

If the data allows, a concept that may help here is *Granger Causality* (Granger, 1969). The essence of Granger Causality is that if a change in X happens before the corresponding change in Y is observed, X may cause Y, and surely not the other way around. It would not make sense the other way around, time can move in but one direction. Practically, it would be a good idea to get data that distinguishes short time periods (relative to the mechanism at hand; a change in technological development or legal conditions would take years, prices of bonds may adjust in seconds) and see if there is a relation between X_t and Y_{t+1}. If a change in X precedes the change in Y, that should become visible if we measure both with small enough time intervals.

Secondly, we should look beyond strict data analysis. Do we have an argument *why* X would be the cause, and Y the effect? if there is causality, there must be some *mechanism* at work. If we cannot identify that mechanism, we should be very weary indeed, since that means the alternative explanation "ah well, this happens by coincidence every now and then" is just as good. In practice, most of the time it isn't too hard to think of several mechanisms that might link X and Y, so if no arguments can be presented, that's quite underwhelming. And if you do have several mechanisms that could potentially link X and Y, try to find variables that are unique to one mechanism, and redo your analysis. That way, you will eventually arrive at both a sound methodology and a convincing argument for your analysis.

There is no causal relationship, but accidents happen.

A significant regression result, however nice, can be an accident. Remember that at a 5% significance level, we have a 5% chance of finding these very numbers even if there is no relationship at all. With p-values close to the 5% level, false conclusions can and will happen. If the p-values are much lower, say 1%, or 0.1%, the chance of this happening is reduced to those amounts.

Beyond this standard caveat, there is also a second type of accident: non stationary data.

Sometimes a variable has a trend; the values in subsequent periods (this phenomenon is limited to time-series data) are related to each other, for example each period, there is a growth of 5%. This is called non-stationary data, as the values continue to grow.

One of the ways to recognize non-stationary is by looking at the average value: if the mean of a bunch of numbers is continuously growing, the data is non stationary. Stationary data will have - as the name suggests - a stationary mean.

Figure 12.1

Example of a non-stationary variable. As time passes, the average value over the last couple of years always goes up. This creates a trend.

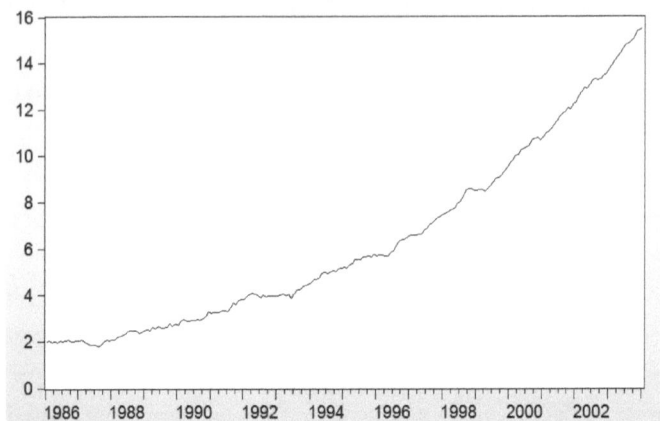

If you regress two variables which have the same trend on each other, you will find a strong relationship. Movements in X and Y will be the same, after all. However, this is not an indication of causality, in fact, *the relation could be equally strong if we switch independent and dependent variable around.*

The trend itself could be seen as an omitted variable. This is perhaps illustrated by the following, somewhat non-business like but telling example regarding non-stationary data:

Suppose that we measure the number of archeological treasure found in an area, and the number of rainbows observed in that area. Despite folkloric tales about leprechauns, there is no relation between the two. Yet is we estimate treasure found as a function of rainbows observed, it might very well be that we find a statistically significant relation! Is there a pot gold at the end of the rainbow after all?

No, it is quite possible that *in our dataset* the two variables move in such a way that such a spurious relationship is found. Why? For the simple fact that both observing a rainbow and digging up treasure are activities that require a human presence. If there are more people around, or with more spare time to become amateur meteorologists or archeologists, that would be a common factor that drives both, as the trend in both variables will be roughly the same.

The good news is that non-stationarity is fixable, see the last section of this chapter. First, let's look at a third scenario.

There is no causal relationship, yet it looks like one - and it's no accident.

It is often possible to show a relationship where it fact none exists; manipulating the data or the analysis with the aim of arriving at a predetermined result is surely as old as data analysis itself. The first line of defense against being duped this way is asking the right questions.

The first question should be: "what is your sample?"

A bad sample is often enough a deliberate attempt to show something that isn't there, and it's done by taking a period where the correlation between X and Y is high, and excluding other periods. This trick isn't too hard to pull off if you have enough different ways to measure roughly the same (say, sales to customers in the 20 to 25 bracket, or the 22 to 27 bracket, or the 24 to 29 bracket, and so on - there will be at least one series that behaves as desired by chance if you look hard enough). The more noise there is in the data, the easier this will be. It of course seriously misrepresents the real situation - and that may be exactly the point.

As for other ways to prevent being duped into accepting a false relationship, the second and third questions should be: "which variables did you include?" and "how did you process the data?". All the methodological problems that cause either a bias in your coefficients or increase the p-values might be abused. See parts III and IV for more detail.

Data analysis with causality in mind: practical steps

So several situations may lead to a false suggestion of a (causal) relation. Neither chance nor a bad sample can be fixed outright; one compensates for this by taking care of the factors that drive your standard errors (see Chapter 4) and using all data which seems reliable, no more and no less.

All the other situations will benefit from proper handling of your data. I'd suggest the following step-by-step approach:

1. Check if you have accounted for all trends. Non-stationarity, is fixable by adjusting your regression.

In order to test for non-stationarity, one can use several tests. Primary candidates are the ADF test and the KPSS test, both are implemented in EVIEWS under the header 'unit root tests'. It is recommended to perform both of these tests, and if one of them indicates a unit root (i.e., non-stationarity), to make the correction explained below. Note that not every unit root test has the same null hypothesis; read the output carefully!

You can fix a non-stationarity problem (also referred to as a unit root or I(1) series in the literature) by taking *first differences*. This means that instead of using the variable itself, we use the change in a variable. So rather than $X_{1,t}$ and $X_{1,t+1}$, we have one observation $X_{1,t+1}-X_{1,t}$. In other words, we use the growth as a variable, and we loose one observation this way (if you variable has dozens or hundreds of observations, this is a small price to pay). We could also look at the relative difference, for example in the return on an investment, which is defined as the change in value divided by the initial investment: $P_{end}-P_{begin}/P_{begin}$.

As any trend will simply become a constant rather than a growth rate in such a set-up, we can proceed as usual with our regression after taking first differences. Theoretically a trend could still remain, but this is very rare in real-life data.

2. Check if your model didn't omit any variables, especially those that could drive both your dependent (Y) and independent (X) variables. Make sure you have modeled seasonal effects explicitly as well. See Chapter 6 on dummies and Chapter 8 on omitted variables.

3. If you're worried about causality, test for Granger causality. In EVIEWS, this is done pairwise, meaning that you check if a variable 'Granger causes' another and vice versa. (Just open your data as a group, so several variables at once. Granger causality tests are then included under 'view'). Be careful with interpreting this information, as Granger causality does *not* imply there is a significant coefficient in a regression (which uses observations from *the same moment in time*), nor does it take into account that there may be several omitted variables that might be the true 'cause'.

4. Always check if you can actually make an argument why this relation should exist. (see Chapter 13, point 4).

13. A final checklist

Congratulations! You now have a toolkit that will allow you to analyze data yourself, but also to ask the right questions if someone else does the analysis. At this stage, a few remarks about what regression analysis can and cannot do for you are in order. If they seem like open doors to you after reading this book, its message has been well received; yet a recap at the end never hurts.

The five evergreens of data analysis:

1 If the data isn't there, no amount of methodology is going to offer a substantial improvement. It's data analysis, and we need the raw input. If we have too few observations, or if they are unreliable or otherwise of poor quality, no meaningful analysis is possible. Even if we manage to get coefficients, their reliability will be low, their standard errors will be high. Always ask for some descriptive statistics of the input data, and check if they make sense. It is possible to find gems hidden in big datasets, it is not possible to draw reliable conclusions based on just a handful of observations.

2 Ask yourself: "Why? Why is this the case? Why do we do it like this?" Not only when it comes to your chose of method, but also your choice of independent variables. Never do something without having some sort of justification ready. That will not just arm you against critique, it will force you to consider alternatives and therefore strengthen your case. You can find relations everywhere, regression analysis does a fine job in that respect. It's your job to make sure you find relations that are meaningful.

3 Check if your results are robust. In truth, there are often many ways to do (roughly) the same thing. You can have a database of consumers that has their marital status as a variable, or the size of their household. Variables like those will overlap (in some age brackets more than in others), even though they will certainly not be identical. If you don't know which variable is the better, try both, but not at the same time (due to multicollinearity). If the results are pointing in the same direction no matter which choice you made, they are robust. That means you can cross off that choice from your list of worries.

4 Ask yourself: "Do I have an answer to my question?" In many cases, it's easy to run a regression, focus on the technical aspects - and you should get them right! - and stop once you have coefficients. But do you understand what's going on? Do you have numbers, or do you have something you can influence or predict, something that tells you what to do next?

The quickest test for this is whether your output makes sense. If you can give an argument *why* this output is plausible, you've got the beginning of a solution - a forecast, a variable that can be changed by your actions perhaps - because you have a *mechanism* to go along with the numbers that tell you strength and reliability.

 If that argument is absent, if there's no reason why the world should be like this, that means you either have work to do trying to make sense of the actual situation, or stumbled across a case of bad luck - regression analysis can never rule out coincidences altogether.

5 Double-check against pitfalls. Regression analysis will only work if the assumptions of the Gauss-Markov-Theorem are met. Use the overview on the next page to see what can go wrong, how to test for it, and most importantly, how to fix it.

Now, let's get to work - implement it!

Appendices

OLS Assumptions

The table below gives an overview of the assumptions of the Gauss-Markov Theorem. If these assumptions are met, regression analysis can be used. If not, a fix is required.

Assumption	Consequences	Diagnosis	Remedy
All relevant variables are included in the model: no variables are missing, categorical data has appropriate dummies, non-linearities are linearized.	Bias in your coefficients. Because of this: standard errors and R^2 also biased.	Include a candidate for an omitted variable, and test if it's significant	Adjust your regression model
No variables are redundant.	Higher standard errors for all variables that are correlated with the redundant variable. No effect on coefficients or R^2.	Single variable: t-test ; multiple variables: F-test, preferably re-do the test after reducing multicollinearity issues.	Throw out any redundant variables that you can isolate (that are individually insignificant)
Homoskedasticity; variance of the residuals is constant	Bias in standard errors, everything else unaffected	White test	White- or Newey-West algorithms in Eviews.
No serial correlation; meaning residuals are uncorrelated with residuals from previous periods	Bias in standard errors, everything else unaffected	Breusch-Godfrey LM test	Newey-West algorithm in Eviews.
Input data is free of random errors.	Bias in coefficients, the estimation procedure is inconsistent. Standard errors biased due to the bias in coefficients	None, unless you have an alternative dataset you know is error-free. In that case, just use that one.	See diagnosis. Take preventative measures to control the problem as much as possible.
All independent variables are exogenous; i.e. not influenced by the dependent ones; (the independent variables are uncorrelated with the residuals)	Bias in coefficients, estimation procedure is inconsistent. Standard errors biased as a result.	Hausmann-test (an F-test using instrumental variables; if they are jointly significant there is endogeneity or misspecification)	The use of instrumental variables, preferably in a Two-stage least Squares regression (2SLS)

Glossary

Part I

Variables:	Variables represent a certain piece of information for each observation, for example how much profit we made in a given period. This information needs to be quantifiable, and cannot have the same value for all observations.
Standard error (simple):	A measure of reliability; the bigger the standard error, the larger the chance that the true value deviates from what we find, and therefore the lower the reliability of our results. See chapter 4 for an extended explanation.
Formula :	The mathematical expression of a relation. On the left-hand side of the equality sign we usually place what we want to explain, on the right-hand side the elements that provide the explanation - this are almost always several terms. For example: $y = a + b*x + e$, but also profit = revenue - costs. Also called equation.
Variable:	A series of numbers, indicating a certain phenomenon, for example annual profits.
Dependent variable:	In a regression, the variable we seek to explain. It's on the left-hand side of the equality sign in a formula; $y = ...$ (y is also its customary symbol). There's always just one of these in a standard regression model.
Independent variable:	In a regression, a variable we use to explain the movements in the dependent variable. The assumption is that changes in the independent variable cause changes in the dependent variable. We can have several in a regression. Commonly denoted X (with a subscript number if there are several, so x_1, x_2 etc.). Also called 'regressors', explanatory variables, or 'x-variables'.
Intercept:	The constant element in a regression. It may be the case all independent variables are zero, but the

dependent one is not (on average). We need a term to make up the difference. Since this point would be the intercept of the regression line with the vertical axis, it's called the intercept. It is the symbol 'a' in y = a +b*x+e

Slope coefficients: The numbers that indicate how strong the impact of an independent variable is. The x-variable is multiplied by a slope-coefficient; if the slope is zero, there's no impact at all, if it's any other number, there is. NB: the intercept and the slope coefficients taken together are often referred to as 'coefficients' or 'parameters. It is the symbol 'b' in y = a +b*x+e.

Residuals: The difference, for each observation, between what we want to explain (the dependent variable) and the combined effect of independent variables and coefficients. So in effect, it's the part of y that we cannot explain. Customary symbol: ε or e.

Sum of squared errors : We take each residual, square it (to eliminate negative values), and add them up. The larger this number is, the worse your model performs in explaining your dependent variable. The aim of regression analysis is to minimize the sum of squared errors.

Part II

EVIEWS: Specialized software to conduct regressions, offering many necessary features without being prohibitively time-consuming to use. All copyrights belong to IHS.

Workfile: The file EVIEWS uses to store all data, but also all output. Each variable is listed separately (called a 'series'), and if the output is saved ('named') it will appear here as well.

Coefficient: A number indicating the influence of an independent variable (in case of a slope-coefficient) or the value of the constant (see intercept)

Standard error:	A measure of reliability of a coefficient, and the square root of the variance of that coefficient. The lower the standard error (relative to the coefficient), the more reliable it is. Also see t-test.
Variance:	The spread around the mean (average value) of a variable or residual series. It's calculated by taking the deviation from the mean for each observation, squaring this value, and taking the average of the resulting numbers.
t-test:	A test for a single null-hypothesis, to see if a coefficient (slope- or intercept-) could have a true value equal to that null-hypothesis. If the t-score is low, the null-hypothesis isn't rejected, and we assume the null-hypothesis is true.
t-score:	The value we get when you take the coefficient, subtract the value it should have under the null-hypothesis, and divide by the standard error. This number can be compared to a table with values of the student's -t distribution, so we can attach a probability to it. (that's the probability of finding that number if the null-hypothesis holds true)
p-value: or Probability:	Also known as 'probability' or 'prob' in EVIEWS output. The chance that, if the null-hypothesis were true, we would find numbers as far away (or further) from the null-hypothesis as our estimates are. If this value is below the significance level, we reject the null-hypothesis.
Null-hypothesis	The condition we want to test, for example that a slope-coefficient is equal to a certain value. If we cannot find enough evidence to reject a null-hypothesis, we assume it's true.
Significance level:	The threshold we use to determine if there is enough evidence against the null-hypothesis. If the significance level is 5%, we accept that there is a 5% chance that when we reject the null-hypothesis, we do so wrongly. Customary levels are 5% (most common), 10% and 1%.

R^2 (R-squared)	Goodness-of-fit measure. Has values between 0 and 1 (if a constant is part fo the model), and can be seen as how much of the variance in y the model explains; an R^2 of 1.00 corresponds to 100% explanation, an R^2 of 0 to 0%.
Logarithmic transformation:	Taking the logarithm of a variable; this means that all observations are replaced by the number we have to raise the base (either 10 or e, which is 2.712) to get the original number. For example, the 10 log of 1000 equals 3, as 10 raised to the third power is 10*10*10=1000
Quadratic transformation:	Taking the square of a variable, by multiplying each observation by itself. It means the result will consist of only positive values, and large numbers become disproportionally larger still.
Taylor's theorem:	Theorem that proves that if you use enough higher order terms (quadratic transformation, cubed, 4th power and so on) together, you can mimick any non-linear relation [over a limited interval] with a linear combination of those higher order terms.
Multicollinearity:	Two or more variables that are correlated and all included as independent variables in your regression. This reduces the precision at which coefficients can be estimated (i.e., it increases standard errors)
Perfect multicollinearity:	Multicollinearity, but now between two (or more) variables that have a correlation coefficient of -1 or +1. This means they contain the same information, and a regression with both as independent variables cannot be estimated.
F-test:	A test for multiple null-hypothesis at the same time, which allows us to test for joint significance (i.e., that all restrictions given by the null-hypotheses hold at the same time)
Wald test:	A generalized version of the F-test; EVIEWS uses this name and produces an F-statistic as part of the output.

Restricted model:	In an F-test, the model where the null-hypotheses are imposed on the regression (so the coefficients are fixed in accordance with the null). This worsens the model relative to the unrestricted model, and this difference is a major input of the F-test)
Correlated:	A correlation coefficient is a measure of the extent to which two variables move together. If a correlation coefficient equals 1, every time one variable goes up, the other will increase as well, and if one member of the pair goes down, the other will so do. if the correlation is -1, they move in opposite directions, if it is zero, there's no telling how one will move based on information about the other variable.
Specification:	The choice about which variables (and with which transformation, if applicable) will be included in your regression.
Auxiliary regression:	A regression that aims to establish the relation between variables which are all independent variables in the main model. For this we need a second regression, where one of these variables is now the dependent (y) variable. The higher the R^2 of an auxiliary regression, the more the variable on the left hand-side of the auxiliary regression is correlated with those on the right-hand side.
Dummy variable:	A variable that can take on only two values: 0 or 1. The '1' indicates the observation belongs to a certain category, the '0' tells you when it doesn't.
Intercept dummy (coefficient):	The coefficient that is multiplied by a dummy variable in an equation, and takes on the role of an additional intercept for the category where the dummy equals 1. The 'a_2' in $Y = (a_1 + a_2*dummy) + (b_1 + b_2*dummy) * X + e$
Slope dummy (coefficient):	Coefficients that are multiplied by a dummy variable in an equation, and take on the role of an additional slope coefficients for the category where the dummy equals 1. The 'b_2' in $Y = (a_1 + a_2*dummy) + (b_1 + b_2 *dummy)* X + e$

Base case:	The basis for comparison in a regression with dummies (according to the changes specification). All dummy coefficients will indicate changes relative to this category, so it's the category for which all dummy variables are zero.
Level specification:	A way to incorporate dummies in your regression with specifying a base case. Formulas will be a variation on $Y = (a_1 *\text{dummy}_1 + a_2*\text{dummy}_2) + (b_1*\text{dummy}_1 + b_2 *\text{dummy}_2)* X + e$
Changes specification:	The way to use dummies as explained in chapter 6, by using a base case. The formula is of the form $Y = (a_1 + a_2*\text{dummy}) + (b_1 + b_2 *\text{dummy})* X + e$

Part III

OLS method:	Ordinary least squares, the standard method for estimating regressions.
Homoskedasticity:	The situation where the variance of your residuals is the same throughout your regression. This means all observations/periods are equally reliable.
Hetero-skedasticity:	The opposite of homoskedasticity; the variance of your residuals is *not* constant. This causes bias in your standard errors.
Serial correlation:	Occurs when one residual is related to the next, for example after a positive residual it's more like to have another positive residual. Often caused by seasonal patterns; it biases your standard errors.
Endogeneity:	A chicken-and-egg situation where X influences Y (as it should), but there's a simultaneous influence of Y on X. Your independent variable is tehrefore not truely independent, and this can cause inconsistency and bias in your coefficients
Gauss-Markov Theorem:	The theory that proves that OLS is BLUE if the assumptions mentioned in part III are met.
Bias:	The situation that the coefficients we find - on average - are not the same as their real value. The difference between our average estimates and the true value is the bias.

BLUE:	Best Linear Unbiased Estimator. A linear estimation procedure (so the relation is a straight line) that produces coefficients that are efficient (lowest possible variance) and unbiased. OLS meets this criterium if the Gauss-Markov theorem holds.
Efficiency:	Characteristic on an estimation procedure. The situation where your estimation is as precise as possible given the information you have; that is, the standard errors are as low as they can be.
Consistency:	Characteristic on an estimation procedure. Do we get the right (true) value for our coefficients if we add ever more data to our estimation? If so, the estimation procedure is consistent.

Part IV

Specification:	The model you use for your regression: which variables do you include? Also incorporates the use of dummies and transformations.
Omitted variable bias:	Bias (in your coefficients) caused by omitting a relevant variable from your model. Occurs if the omitted variable is correlated with the included variables.
Structural break:	A dividing point in your dataset with a different relation between X and Y before the structural break than after.
Mean Squared Error: (MSE) criterion	A way to compare models with different levels of bias and standard errors. Per variable, take the bias, square it, and add the variance (square of the standard error). The lower the MSE, the better.
Redundant variable:	A variable that doesn't add enouh to the explanatory power of a regression to merit its inclusion in the model. Judged by looking at the coefficient; if it doesn't differ significantly from zero (i.e. p-value below 5%), it's redundant.
Homoskedasticity	The situation where all residuals have the same variance, and therefore are equally reliable. OLS assumes this. The opposite is heteroskedasticity.

Hetero-skedasticity:	The situation where your residuals have a non-constant variance (for example, the spread of your residuals increases over time). Not every residual is as reliable, which biases the standard errors unless corrected
Serial correlation:	A situation where one residual contains information about earlier (or later) residuals as well. Formally, the correlation between residuals in period t and an earlier period are not equal to zero. OLS only provides correct results if there is no serial correlation, as it affects the standard errors.
White-test:	A diagnostic test for homoskedasticity. The null-hypothesis is that the variance of the residuals can only be explained by a constant (so null = homoskedasticity), if we reject that using an auxiliary regression and an F-test, we say the regression suffers from heteroskedasticity.
Chi-square distribution:	A statistical distribution that can be used to judge if the R^2 of an auxiliary regression is significantly different from zero.
White-algorithm:	A set of calculations that will produce standard errors that are corrected for heteroskedasticity. NB: it does not affect the coefficients nor the residuals, only the standard errors of your original regression.
Newey-West algorithm:	A more advanced version of the White algorithm that also corrects for serial correlation.
Breusch-Godfrey LM -test:	The diagnostic test used to detect serial correlation. The user can specifiy how many lags should be included (i.e., how far back the supposed relation between residuals would go)
Durbin-Watson (DW)-test:	A 'quick and dirty' test for serial correlation. Will only detect first order serial correlation, is unsuited for patterns that go back further in time. Unlike most test, a p-value is not reported; values between 1,5 and 2,5 are supposed to be free from serial correlation.

White test:	The diagnostic test used to detect heteroskedasticity.
Endogeneity:	The situation where there is dual causality: X influences Y, and Y influences X. This causes a correlation between independent variables and residuals, which in turn is responsible for biased coefficients (and inconsistency).
Instrumental variables:	A variable, or set of variables, that approximate the variable tainted by endogeneity. It is hoped the approximation is good enough to extract meaningful results.
Errors-in-variables:	The situation where your variables aren't accurately measured, allowing for a discrepancy between their true values and the ones in your dataset.
Exogeneous variable:	An explanatory variable not affected by an endogeneity problem: there is no element in the model that influences this variable, it's truly independent.
Endogeneous variable:	A variable that does suffer from endogeneity, some other factor - that could be modelled - determines it in whole or in part.

Part V

Forecasting:	Predicting future values of a variable using a relationship, for example one established thorugh regression analysis.
Autoregression:	A regression where the current value of a variable is determined by observations for the same vaariable, but in previous periods.
Hold-out sample:	Part of your dataset that is not used to estimate the model that produces the forecast, but set aside to check whether the forecasts are accurate enough.
RMSE:	Root Mean Square Error. Take your prediction errors, square them, average them, and take a square root again. An indication for the relative predictive power of a forecasting model. A lower

RMSE is better.

MAD: Mean Absolute Deviation. Take your forecasting errors, drop any minus signs, and average. Another indication for predictive power, lower is again better.

Causality: The situation where an independent variable causes a change in a dependent variable. Strictly speaking, this cannot be proven with regression analysis, as only correlations are enough for significant coefficients.

Granger Causality: Something close to causality, but not quite - yet this can be empirically proven. Occurs if the change in independent variable precedes the change in dependent variable in time.

Non-stationarity: A situation where a variable has a trend, usually over time. If two non-stationary variables that share a trend are regressed on each other, the coefficients as well as their reliability will seem to be much higher than they are in reality.

ADF test / Tests for a unit root, that is, tests that will indicate if your variable is non-stationary. If the unit root is

KPSS test: present, non-stationarity should be adressed by taking first differences.

First differences: Instead of using the variable itself, we use the change in a variable. So rather than $X_{1,t}$ and $X_{1,t+1}$, we have one observation $X_{1,t+1}-X_{1,t}$. In other words, we use the growth as a variable. We could also look at the relative difference, for example in the return on an investment, which is defined as the change in value divided by the initial investment: $P_{end}-P_{begin}/P_{begin}$.

Overview of diagnostic tests

In all cases, reject your null-hypothesis if the probability is below 5%. Otherwise, accept the null hypothesis!

Diagnostic test	Purpose	Null-hypothesis	Example of the null-hypothesis
T-test (standard eviews output)	Test if a variable belongs in the model.	coefficient = 0	C(2)=0
T-test (general)	Test if a variable is significantly different from a pre-specified value (your null-hypothesis).	coefficient = prespecified value	C(3)=25
F-test	Test if two or variables have a certain value *at the same time*. Also useful to test if two variables can be removed form the model *simultanously*.	coefficient$_A$ = value 1, coefficient$_B$ = value 2.	C(1)=0, C(2)=0
Durbin-Watson test	Test if the residuals are affected by first order serial correlation	no first order serial correlation, rho$_1$ = 0	in $e_t = \rho e_{t-1} + u_t$ $\rho = 0$
Breusch-Godfrey LM test	Test if the residuals are affected by any order serial correlation the user sets	no serial correlation, all rho's = 0	$\rho_1 = 0$ and $\rho_2 = 0$, in $e_t = \rho_1 e_{t-1} + \rho_2 e_{t-2} + u_t$
White-test	Test if the residuals are affected by hetero-skedasticity	No hetero-skedasticity	The variables explaining resid^2 (squared residuals) are not jointly significant.

ABOUT THE AUTHOR

Philippe Versijp (1980) is lecturer in Finance at the University of Amsterdam and owner of Covariance, a company specializing in teaching and advice.

He obtained his MSc and PhD at Erasmus University Rotterdam, specializing in innovative ways to model risk on stock markets. Later his focus shifted from research to teaching: he lists making complex issues understandable as his passion. He was awarded the Top Lecturer Award 2010 at Erasmus.

His audiences range from bachelor students to MBAs; he has extensive experience in post-experience programs in Amsterdam, Rotterdam and Curaçao.